# MYSTICAL FLORA

LE BIEN-HEVREVX FRANÇOIS DE SALES EVESQVE DE GENEVE.
Balthasar Moncornet ex.

# MYSTICAL FLORA

OF

### St. Francis de Sales

OR,

## THE CHRISTIAN LIFE
*Under the Emblem of Plants*

Translated by
CLARA MULHOLLAND

With Introduction by
THE MOST REV. GEORGE CONROY, D.D.
*Bishop of Amman and Clonmacnoise*

MEDIATRIX PRESS
MMXXI

ISBN: 978-1-953746-95-5

*The Mystical Flora of St. Francis de Sales* ©Mediatrix Press, 2021.

All rights reserved. With the exception of short excerpts used in critical review, no part of this work may be reproduced, transmitted or stored in any form whatsoever, without the prior written permission of the publisher.

This work has been derived, edited and arranged from *The Mystical Flora of St. Francis*, first published in 1876. The typography and editorial changes in this edition are the property of Mediatrix Press, and may not be reproduced, in whole or in part, physically or electronically without written permission from the publisher.

Published in the United States by

Mediatrix Press
607 E 6th Ave.
Post Falls, ID 83854
www.mediatrixpress.com

# Table of Contents

INTRODUCTION ix

## I. GENERAL NOTIONS
1. *Principles and Characteristics of a Christian Life* 1
2. *Sweetness and Advantages of a Christian Life.* 6

## II. OBSTACLES TO A CHRISTIAN LIFE
1. *Sin.* 9
2. *Attachment to Sin and Imperfections* 14
3. *Useless Affections and Desires* 17

## III. PURIFICATION OF THE SOUL
Its Necessity and its Principles. 21

## IV. PRACTICE OF A CHRISTIAN LIFE
1. *Faults to be fought against or avoided.* 29
2. *Virtues in General* 36
3. *On Virtues in Particular.* 44
    Humility and Obedience 44
    Chastity 48
    Charity—Simplicity—Sweetness 52
    Patience 54
    Little Virtues 55

## V. PIOUS EXERCISES OF A CHRISTIAN LIFE 59
1. *Prayer, Meditation, and the Word of God.* 59
2. *Devotion to our Lady and to the Saints.* 67
3. *Meditation upon the Mysteries of the Life of Our Lord and his Blessed Mother, our Lady.* 71

    4. *Sacraments.*                                       93
        Confirmation                        93
        Penance                             93
        Eucharist                           94
        The Holy Mass                96
        Marriage                            96

VI. TRIALS OF A CHRISTIAN LIFE
    1. *Tribulations.*                            99
    2. *Spiritual Desolations.*             104

VII. DIVINE LOVE: ITS NOBLE PREROGATIVES AND
     SUBLIME ASPIRATIONS
    1. *Nature, Properties, and Object of Divine Love.*
                                                             109
    2. *Marvelous Effects of Divine Love.*    113
    3. *Mystical Transports of Divine Love.*   122
    4. *Consolations and Promises if Divine Love.*  130

# INTRODUCTION

"GOD," says St. Thomas Aquinas, "like the excellent master that He is, has taken care to provide us with writings of the best kind. 'What things soever were written,' He tells us, 'were written for our learning.' Now, these writings are comprised in two books—that is to say, in the Book of Creation and in the Book of Scripture. The first of these books has as many most perfect writings as it has creatures, and these writings teach us the truth without a lie." (*Serm. in Dom. II Advent*).

But, men have not always read aright the lessons presented in the book of nature. The first lesson which the world teaches by itself is that it is God's work, for "by the greatness and the beauty of the creature, the Creator of them may be seen, so as to be known thereby" (Wid. 12:5). And yet, how many in all ages have closed their minds those whose ear has listened to the silent voices by which the universe proclaims a God, how many "have imagined either the fire, or the wind, or the swift air, or the circle of the stars, or the sun and moon, to be the gods that rule the world" (*ibid.* v. 3); being fascinated by the thousand lovelinesses of earth into forgetting "how much the Lord of them is more beautiful than they; for the first author of beauty made all these things." Others, again, in the soul's natural recoil from this drear

## The Mystical Flora

materialism, have so spiritualized the sensible beauty of nature as to become themselves the prey of a weak and morbid sentimentalism. This last is a characteristic of English literature in the present century, and its influence on the public mind has been injurious at least in one important respect. The soul it loves to trace in nature is not the soul which the Apostle describes as groaning and travailing in supernatural longing after its own restoration by grace; to the lessons it sets forth from the Book of Creation it sub joins no parallel, though loftier, teachings from the Book of Scripture. Hence it is that the love of nature in our days has gone so far apart from Christian feeling. Men have forgotten that God's thoughts find expression in the visible, as well as in the invisible, world, and that inner and secret harmonies bind the natural and the supernatural together. The things of beauty which God has bidden arise on the earth lose half their grace, because men do not mount by them to the better understanding of the supernal beauty of the operations of that world which Faith reveals to our gaze.

The God who writes his thoughts in the Book of Nature is the same who writes in the Book of Scripture. And those whom He sent to expound to mankind the teachings of the latter have ever loved to illustrate its heavenly doctrine from the pages of the former. At sundry times and in diverse manners He spoke his thoughts in times past by the prophets. Chief of these was Isaiah; and his graphic pen borrows, from all parts of creation, figures that express, with a reality and a force that can never die, the Divine thought of which he was the in spired messenger. And when the line of the

## Introduction

prophets was ended, and His Son had come to reveal His Father's will, He, too, loved to employ the objects belonging to the visible world He Himself had made to describe the secret things He beheld in the bosom of His Father. The spiritual edifice of His Church was as a city built upon a rock; His apostles were the salt of the earth and the light of the world; His faithful were sheep whose Shepherd He was; the history of man's soul was the history of the seed that is sown; His followers were to learn confidence in His Providence from the bird that lives in the air, and from the lilies that neither toil nor spin. And so was it also with the teachers whom He appointed to continue his work. In the writings of the Fathers and Doctors of the Church the eternal truths are continually presented to the mind imaged in comparisons borrowed from natural objects. St. Gregory the Great speaks of the visible creation as bearing upon it traces of the footprints of God, and he describes the world's beauty as a glad smile lighted by its conscious knowledge of its Maker's secrets, and nature's voices as the murmur of Divine truth rising upon the soul from all that lives and moves within the universe. It is the sense of this harmony between the natural and the spiritual worlds that gives its clearness and freshness to the language of the Catholic liturgy; it is the key to the pregnant symbolism of the sacraments. This it is which forms the "right heart," which the author of the "Imitation" tells us "finds in every creature a mirror of life and a book of holy doctrine. To it no creature is so small and vile that it does not show forth the goodness of God."

Few among the Church's writers surpass Francis de

## The Mystical Flora

Sales in the skillful use of comparison drawn from nature to illustrate the operations of grace in the spiritual life. In this he holds a place peculiarly his own. His images do not recall scenes of Cappadocian gloom, like those of St. Basil, nor, like St. Jerome's, the harshness of the desert. But rather as the clear blue waters of the lakes of his own Savoy soften, without distorting, the rugged outlines of the overhanging hills, which they reflect bright with sunshine, joyful with flowers, and crowned with teeming vines, so does his gentle spirit present to our minds the loftiest doctrines in all the grandeur of truth, and yet clothed in images of beauty that charm the fancy, while they flash new light upon the understanding. But most of all is this true of him as he comes in from the garden with hands full of comparisons gathered from the flowers that bloom therein.

So delicate at such times is his taste, so exquisite his choice of language, so refined the analogies he unfolds, that beneath the spell of his words our souls become as vividly conscious of the truth he seeks to convey as our senses would be of the flower of which he speaks, were we to hold its stem in our hands and breathe the fragrance it sheds around. In the Mystical Flora, which is now for the first time offered in an English dress, a loving hand has collected the choicest of St. Francis's spiritual comparisons drawn from plants and flowers. Nor have the specimens been gathered at random. They have been so arranged that they form a perfect treatise on the devout life, from its first principles to its consummation, according to the plan laid down by the Saint himself in his ascetic writings. It is a book that will bring pleasure

*Introduction*

to the lover of nature, as well as profit to the seeker after grace. It exhibits in one of the fairest pages of the Book of Creation, a commentary on one of the most difficult in the Book of Scripture; and whosoever, under the guidance of the Saint, will earnestly study its teaching, cannot fail to learn, with Philothea, "how one may draw good thoughts and holy aspirations from everything that presents itself in all the variety of this mortal life" (*Devout Life*, part II. ch. 13).

✠ GEORGE CONROY,
Bishop of Ardagh and Clonmacnoise.
Longford, Nov. 21, 1876.

## The Vine

# MYSTICAL FLORA

THE PASSION FLOWER

# I.
# GENERAL NOTIONS

## 1. *Principles and Characteristics of a Christian Life*

AM about to tell all those who listen to me, that their souls are God's vineyard, in which faith is the cistern, hope the tower, holy charity the wine press, and the law of God the hedge that separates them from unfaithful people. To you, dear daughter, I say that your will is your vineyard; the Divine inspirations poured into your soul by God, the cistern; holy chastity, the tower, which, like that of David, should be made of ivory; obedience, by which all your actions become meritorious, the winepress. Oh! may God preserve this vineyard which He has planted with his own hand. May He fill the cistern with the abundant waters of Divine grace. May He protect his tower. May his wine-press, beneath the pressure of his hand, teem with good wine. May He always keep the beautiful hedge with which He has surrounded his vineyard close and thick, and may his holy angels be the immortal vine-dressers.

*Letter to Me. De Chantal,* February 21, 1606

## The Mystical Flora

I have seen a tree planted by St. Dominic at Rome.[1] Everybody visits it and loves it for the sake of the planter. Thus having seen the tree of the desire of sanctity planted in your soul by our Lord, I love it dearly, and take the greatest delight in considering it. Now, I exhort you to do likewise, and to say with me, "God grant that you may flourish, O fair plant, nursling of heaven, God grant you may bring to maturity your fruit, and may He preserve it in its ripeness, day and night, from the cruel winds which cast our earthly fruit upon the ground, where wild and hungry animals devour it.

*Letter to St. Chantal*, 21.

The longing for holiness should be like the orange trees of the sea-coast of Genoa, which are covered with fruit, flowers, and leaves nearly all the year round. For your desire should daily ripen into fruit on every occasion of doing good that offers, while it should never cease to yearn after fresh opportunities of advancement. These yearnings are the flowers of the tree; its leaves, the frequent acknowledgment of your own weakness, which preserves both your good works and your good desires.

*Letter to St. Chantal*, 21.

There are many people who, when they think of the goodness of God and the passion of our Savior, are so much overcome that they sigh and weep, with much

---

[1] The saint here alludes to the well known orange tree in the convent of Santa Sabina.

## General Notions

emotion praying and thanking God for his goodness. To see them one would imagine that they were filled with great devotion. Yet, when the moment of trial comes, we find that, like the hot summer rain which falls in thick drops upon the earth, Without penetrating it thoroughly, producing nothing but mushrooms, these tears, falling upon a wicked, sinful heart, without truly penetrating it, are quite useless. In spite of all this sensible devotion, these poor creatures would not part with one farthing of their ill-gotten gains, nor renounce one of their perverse inclinations, nor suffer the slightest inconvenience for the love of the Savior over whom they have wept. So we may say that these feelings of devotion are a kind of spiritual mushroom, which are not only far from being true devotion, but are very often so many snares laid by the devil, who satisfies these souls with small consolations, and thereby hinders them from seeking true and solid devotion, which consists in a constant and resolute will, ever ready to execute whatever we know to be agreeable to God.

*Devout Life,* part IV. ch. 13.

But then, you may say, since there are some feelings of sensible devotion which come from God, and are consequently good, whilst others come either from nature or from the enemy, and are useless, dangerous, and pernicious, how am I to distinguish them and know the bad and useless from the good? As a general rule, my dear Philothea, we must judge the affections and passions of our souls by their fruits.

Our hearts are trees, the affections and passions their

## The Mystical Flora

branches, and their works and actions are their fruit. The heart is good which has good affections, and the affections are good which produce good and holy actions. If sweetness, tenderness, and consolations make us more humble, patient, gentle, charitable, and compassionate towards our neighbor, more fervent in mortifying our concupiscences and evil inclinations, more constant in our religious exercises, more pliable in the hands of our superiors, more simple in our mode of life, then, without doubt, Philothea, they come from God. But if this sweetness be sweetness only for ourselves, making us curious, sour, punctilious, impatient, obstinate, proud, presumptuous, and hard hearted towards our neighbor, making us believe that we are saints, and, as such, beyond the need of direction or of correction; then, most certainly, these consolations are false and pernicious. A good tree bears good fruit.

*Devout Life*, part IV. ch. 13.

A child will weep to see his mother bleed from the touch of a knife. Now, though he has cried for her pain in this way, should she ask from him the sweetmeats or the apple he holds in his hand, he would refuse to give them. Such are, for the most part, our tender devotions. When we think of our Lord's Heart transfixed with a lance, we weep tenderly. Alas! dear Philothea, it is right and just that we should weep over the death and passion of our Father and Redeemer, but why should we refuse to give Him the apple which we hold in our hands, and which He asks from us so often, that is to say, our heart, the one golden apple that our Divine Savior requires of us? Why

## General Notions

do we not renounce, for his sake, these little affections, pleasures, and satisfactions which He wishes to take from us and cannot, because we are so unwilling to give up our sweetmeats which we value more than His celestial grace?

*Devout Life*, part IV. ch. 13.

In the beginning God commanded the plants to bear fruit, each according to its kind; so, in like manner, He commands all Christians, who are the living plants of his Church, to produce the fruits of devotion, each one according to his position and vocation.

*Devout Life*, part I. ch. 3.

Persons who live in towns, or at court, and who by their position are obliged to live, externally at least, as others live, pretend very often that it is impossible to think of leading a spiritual life; they say that, as no animal would dare to taste the seed of the plant known as Palma Christi, so no man should dare to touch the palm of Christian piety so long as he is in the midst of worldly affairs.

Now, I wish to show them that as the mother-of-pearl lives in the sea without tasting a drop of its brine, and as near the Chelidonian Isles there are fountains of pure, fresh water in the midst of the ocean, and as a fire-moth may fly through the flame of a candle without burning its wings, so a strong and faithful soul may live in the midst of the world untouched by its waters, may find springs of true piety in the midst of the bitter waves of

## The Mystical Flora

worldliness, and fly through the flames of earthly covetousness without burning the wings of holy longings and ardent desires for a spiritual life. It is true that this is difficult, and that is the very reason why I wish many persons to labor more ardently and carefully than they have done up to this present time.

*Devout Life*, Preface.

### 2. Sweetness and Advantages of a Christian Life.

It is said that horses and mules laden with figs quickly fall beneath the load. The law of God is lighter and sweeter than figs; but man, who has become "like the horse and the mule, who have no understanding" (Ps. 31:9), loses courage, and has not strength enough to carry this sweet burden.

*Love of God*, book VIII. ch. 5.

On the contrary, as a branch of agnus-castus prevents the traveler who bears it from feeling the fatigue of his journey, so the cross, the mortification, the yoke and law of our Savior, who is the true *chaste lamb*, is a burden which consoles and rejoices the hearts of those who love his Divine Majesty. It is no trouble to toil at a work of love, or if it be a trouble it is a delightful trouble. Toil blended with holy love is a mixture of bitter with sweet, more agreeable to the taste than an unmixed sweetness.

*Love of God, id. id.*

Look at the bees upon the thyme. There they find a bitter juice, but in sucking it they convert it into honey,

## General Notions

because this is their special power. O worldly man! Though it is true that devout souls find much bitterness in their exercises of mortification, nevertheless, in performing them they convert them into sweetness and joy. Fire, flames, wheels, swords, were as flowers and perfumes to the martyrs, because they were truly devout. If devotion can sweeten the cruelest tortures, and even death itself, what will it not do for acts of true virtue? Sugar sweetens unripe fruit, and corrects whatever is harsh or hurtful in that which is quite ripe. Now, devotion is the true spiritual sugar which takes from mortifications their bitterness, and all danger from consolations; it cheers the poor and restrains the rich, it mitigates the misery of the oppressed and the insolence of favorites, the sadness of those in solitude and the dissensions of those who live together. It is like the fire in the winter and the dew in the summer. It knows how to abound and how to want, it makes honor and contempt equally useful. It bears, with even mind, pleasure as well as pain, and fills us with a wonderful sweetness.

*Devout Life*, part 1. ch. 2.

Believe me, dear Philothea, devotion is the very sweetest of all sweets, the queen of virtues, and the perfection of charity. If charity is milk, devotion is its cream. If it is a plant, devotion is its flower; if it is a precious stone, devotion is its brilliancy; if it is a precious balm, devotion is the perfume—a perfume of sweetness which comforts men, and causes the angels to rejoice.

*Devout Life*, id. id.

# THE ROSE

## II.
## OBSTACLES TO A CHRISTIAN LIFE

### 1. *Sin.*

HE magnet, as everyone knows, dear Theotime, attracts and draws iron towards it by a secret and very marvelous virtue. But, nevertheless, five different things hinder this operation: *a)* Too great a distance between the magnet and its object; *b)* the interposition of a diamond; *c)* the presence of grease on the iron; *d)* if the iron has been rubbed with garlic; *e)* if it be too heavy. Our hearts were made for God, who draws them towards Him continually, and never ceases to shed upon them the charms of his celestial love. But five things prevent this holy attraction from operating: *a)* sin which separates us from God; *b)* love of riches; *c)* sensual pleasures; *d)* pride and vanity; *e)* self-love and the multitude of unruly passions which it produces, and which are a heavy, wearisome load that drags and weighs us down.

*Love of God*, book VII. ch. 14.

How is it possible that a rational soul, having once tasted the delights of Divine love, can ever willingly turn to drink the bitter waters of mortal sin? Children who are fed on milk, butter, and honey, detest the bitterness of wormwood and orpine, and cry piteously if they are forced to taste it. How, then, O true God! can a soul that has once tasted its Creator's goodness and love, forsake

## The Mystical Flora

You to follow the vanities of the world?
*Love of God*, book IV. ch. l.

The great St. Augustine set himself one day to consider at his leisure the qualities of the mandrake,[2] in order to find out why Rachel so ardently desired to possess it. He found it beautiful to look at, pleasant to smell, but insipid and without taste or flavor. Now, the ancients relate that when surgeons present its juice to those upon whom they wish to perform an operation, the smell alone is sufficient to render the patients insensible, by casting them into a deep sleep. This is why the mandrake is a charm, which enchants the eyes, and softens pain, sorrow, and all our passions, by sleep. He, however, who inhales the odor for any length of time becomes dumb, and he who drinks of it deeply dies without remedy. Could the pomps, riches, and delectations of worldly men, be better represented, dear Theotime? They are beautiful and attractive, but whoever eats of these apples, that is to say, whoever examines them carefully, will find them without taste or pleasure. Nevertheless, they charm and soothe by their vain odor, and the value put upon them by the children of the world distracts those who enjoy them too much or indulge in them too frequently. Now, it is for mandrake such as this, for vague shadows of contentment, that we leave the love

---

[2] A mandrake is the root of a plant, historically derived either from plants of the genus Mandragora found in the Mediterranean region, or from other species, such as Bryonia alba, the English mandrake, which have similar properties.

of our celestial Spouse. And how can we say that we love Him above all things when we prefer these miserable vanities to his Divine grace?

*Love of God*, book X. ch. 9.

The lake, which profane writers call Asphaltite, and sacred authors the Dead Sea, is so cursed that nothing can live in its waters. When the fish from the river Jordan approach it, they die instantaneously, if they do not turn back and retrace their course against the stream. The trees on its banks produce nothing living, for although their fruits look much the same as those of other countries, yet, when plucked, they are found to be but rinds full of dust that flies off with the wind. This is a monument of the most infamous sins, in punishment of which this country, with its four well populated cities, was reduced to being a place of putrefaction and infection. Nothing can more clearly show us the evil of sin than this abominable lake, which originated in the most execrable wickedness that man could commit. Sin, then, like a dead and death-giving sea, kills everyone who falls into it. A soul in which it dwells can give birth to nothing living, nor can anything living grow upon its banks. O my God! Nothing, dear Theotime; for not only is sin a dead work in itself, but it is so pestilent and venomous that the most excellent virtues belonging to a soul in sin are without fruit, and although sometimes the acts of persons in sin resemble the acts of those in grace, yet they are but rinds filled with dust, which are rewarded by God with temporal blessings, but can never be relished by his justice, so as to receive an eternal reward in the kingdom of God's glory. They wither and perish upon the trees that bore them, nor can they be held in God's hand, being empty and without value, as was said in the Apocalypse of the bishop of Sardis, who had the name of being alive because of the virtues he practiced, whereas he was dead (Apoc. 3:1), because being in sin they were not living fruits but empty skins, pleasing to the eye, yet unwholesome to eat. So we may all say with the apostle, "If I have not charity I am nothing" (1 Cor. 13:2); and with St. Augustine, " Fill a heart with charity, and all is well; take away this charity, and nothing is of value." That is to say, nothing is of any value towards gaining our eternal reward, for, as I said before, good works and acts of virtue performed by sinners are rewarded by God in a temporal manner; but, then, Theotime, my friend, "What does it profit a man if he gains the whole world and suffer the loss of his own soul ?" (Matt. 26:26.)

*Love of God*, book XI. ch. 11.

We may say that a dead faith is like a dry tree, without sap or vitality, and which therefore, when the spring-time comes round and the other trees put forth leaves and flowers, remains bare and without fruit, because it lacks the vital sap which runs in every tree that lives even though it may seem dead. And although during the winter months they too appeared dead like it, the life and sap within them now burst forth, and they become fresh and beautiful to look at, whilst the dead tree remains bare. It is a tree like the rest, it is true; but alas! it is dry, and will never more bear leaves, or fruit, or

flowers. So, it is with a dead faith, which can never bear the fruit and flowers of good deeds, which a living faith bears at all times and seasons. It is, therefore, by the operations of charity that we know whether faith is living, dead, or dying; and when it produces no good actions we say it is a dead faith; when these actions are weak and few, we say it is dying; whereas, if, on the contrary, they are frequent and fervent, we say that it is a living faith. Oh, how truly beautiful is this living faith!
*Sermon for the Thursday in the Second Week of Lent.*

When we see a tree blown about by the storm, stripped of its fruit and leaves, we say that it has lost all, because, although the tree itself is intact, we know that it is now without fruit. So, in like manner, when our charity is overcome by our attachment to venial sins, we say that it is weakened and enfeebled, not because the habit of charity has ceased to be entire in our hearts, but because it is without the works which are its fruits.
*Love of God*, book IV. ch. 2.

You should certainly try to correct these faults, because they are small, and because the best time to combat them is while they are small; for if you wait until they grow, it will be more difficult to overcome them. It is easy to change the course of a river near its source, where it is yet a scanty streamlet, but farther down it mocks your efforts. "Catch us the little foxes that destroy the vines" (Cant. 2:15). They are small, do not wait for them to grow large. If you do, it will not only be difficult to stop them, but when you wish to do so, you will find

## The Mystical Flora

that they have already spoiled everything.
*Letter to the Community of the Daughters of God,* Nov. 22, 1602.

The worm that gnawed at the gourd belonging to Jonah seemed very small, but its malice was so great that the shrub perished. The faults of your community appear trifling, but their malice is so great that it injures your vow of poverty.
*Same letter.*

### 2. Attachment to Sin and Imperfections.

All the Israelites came forth from the land of Egypt, but they did not all come forth in heart, and so a great number of them murmured and sighed for the flesh-pots of Egypt. So it is with a great many penitents who renounce their sins, but renounce not the affection for sin; that is to say, they resolve never to sin again, but they are vexed at having to give up the unhappy delectations of sin. They renounce sin, and withdraw from it, but they look back longingly towards it, as Lot's wife looked back upon Sodom.
*Devout Life,* part I. ch. 7.

They abstain from sin as a sick man abstains from melons, when told by the physician that if he eats them he will die. Yet, he still longs for them, and bargains for them, and wishes at least to smell them, and envies those who are permitted to eat them. So, weak and feeble penitents abstain from sin for some time, but it is with regret, and they would be glad to sin if they could do so

## Obstacles to a Christian Life

without being damned. They speak of sin with feeling and zest, and think those happy who commit it.
*Devout Life*, part I. ch. 7.

A man who has determined upon revenge, will give up his design at confession. But you will soon find him in the midst of his friends taking pleasure in talking of his quarrel, and saying that, if it were not for the fear of God he would have done this, that, or the other. He will add that the Divine law of forgiving our enemies is hard, and that he wishes to God it were lawful to revenge ourselves. Who can doubt that this poor man, although he has renounced his sin, is nevertheless attached to it? Although he has indeed left the land of Egypt, yet he is there in heart, still longing for the flesh-pots which he used to partake of. It is the same case with a woman, who, professing to detest her wicked loves, is nevertheless pleased to be courted and attended by them. Alas! such persons are in terrible danger.
*Ibid.*

I do not mean to say, dear Theotime, that there are not some passions in man which, as the mistletoe comes upon the tree by way of overgrowth and as a parasite, are born in the very midst of love, and round about love, but nevertheless are not love, nor part of love, but superfluities, which are not only of no use towards the maintenance or perfecting of love, but injure it and weaken it; so much so, that if they be not removed they will certainly destroy it altogether.
*Love of God*, book I. ch. 2.

## The Mystical Flora

How is it possible, my daughter, that, with such a will to love God, so many imperfections appear and grow up within me? They do not come of my own will, nor by my will. No, most certainly not! They spring up, it seems to me, like the mistletoe which grows upon the tree, but is no part of the tree.

*Letter, July 14, 1615.*

It sometimes happens that even souls who have attained a singular and perfect love fall into great imperfections and venial sins. There were bitter disputes between great servants of God, yes, even between some of the divine apostles, who, we cannot deny, fell into many imperfections, by which charity was not, it is true, violated, but lessened in its fervor. Now, although these great souls ordinarily loved God with a love perfectly pure, yet we cannot say that they were in a state of perfect charity. For, as we see that good trees never produce bad or rotten fruit, still they do sometimes bear fruit that is green or eaten by mistletoe or moss; so, great saints, although they never commit mortal sins, sometimes do useless, rude, or unkind actions, and then we must confess that these trees are fruitful, otherwise they would not be good, still we cannot deny that some of their fruits are unfruitful, for who can deny that the mistletoe on trees is an unfruitful fruit? And who will deny that little tempers, bursts of laughter and excessive joy, movements of vanity and feelings of contempt, are not useless and illegitimate passions? And, nevertheless, the just man shall fall seven times, that is to say very

often.
*Love of God*, book IX. ch. 5.

### 3. Useless Affections and Desires.

The lily has no regular season, but flowers early or late, according to the depth of earth in which we plant it. For if planted but three fingers deep it flowers immediately, but if six or nine fingers deep it is later in proportion. In like manner, if a soul who wishes to love God is plunged deeply in worldly affairs, it will be a very long time before it flowers. But if it lives in the world only as much as its state requires, then you will see it put forth beautiful flowers and spread sweet perfume all around.
*Love of God*, book XII. ch. 3.

When St. John's disciples had departed, our Lord turned to the people who followed Him, saying, "What went you out into the desert to see? A reed shaken by the wind!" Oh, no! St. John was certainly not a reed, weak and inconstant, for he was always firm and unshaken in the midst of the storms and tempests of tribulation. But as for us, we are in truth very changeable, so much so that we seem to bend and sway with each change of the season; We are inconstant reeds carried away by our evil inclinations and passions.
*Sermon for the Second Sunday of Advent.*

## The Mystical Flora

We are likely to imitate the cravings of women in poor health, who long for fresh cherries in autumn and fresh grapes in spring. I do not approve of any person, who has a particular duty or vocation, desiring any kind of life but that which agrees with his obligations, or any exercises incompatible with his present condition. Otherwise, he is sure to be dissipated and careless in performing his necessary duties.

*Devout Life*, part III. ch. 3.

How do you think it happens, dear Theotime, that in the spring dogs lose the scent and track of an animal more easily than at any other time of the year? Men and philosophers say that it is because at that time the herbs and flowers are in their full bloom, and the variety of their perfumes so deadens the dogs' senses, that they cannot distinguish between the scent of the flowers and the scent of their prey. Certainly, those souls who are continually filled with worldly desires, designs, and projects, never long for Divine and celestial love, nor can they follow the loving footsteps of the Divine Love who is compared to the roe or the young hart (Cant. 2:9).

*Love of God*, book XII. ch. 3.

The List

The Lily

## III.
## PURIFICATION OF THE SOUL

*Its Necessity and its Principles.*

HE Divine Spouse in the Canticles says, "The flowers have appeared in our land, the time of pruning is come." What are the flowers of our hearts, O Philothea, if not our holy desires? Now, as soon as they appear, we must put our hand to the pruning-hook, and cut away from our conscience all that is dead and useless.

*Devout Life*, part I. ch. 5.

There are some persons who are naturally light and frivolous; others sharp and waspish; others tenacious of their own opinions; others inclined to anger and indignation; in fact, there are very few persons in whom we do not find some kind of imperfections. But though such faults may appear to be natural to each one, yet they may be corrected and moderated, and with great care and by cultivating the opposite virtue we may free ourselves from them altogether. And I tell you, Philothea, that this must be done. Ways have been found to change bitter almonds into sweet, merely by piercing the foot of the tree so as to let the juice run out. Why can we not expel our perverse inclinations and so become better? There is no natural character so good that it cannot be made bad by vicious habits. Likewise, there is none so averse that it cannot be subdued, first, by the grace of God, then by industry and diligence.

Devout Life, part 1. ch. 4.

To renounce ourselves is simply to purify ourselves from everything that is done through the instinct of self-love. So long as we are in this mortal life, it will not fail to produce off-shoots, which should be immediately cut away, just like a vine. And as it is not sufficient to trim the vine once a year, but it must be cut at one time and at another stripped of its leaves, likewise the vine-dresser must have the pruning hook continually ready to cut off the useless shoots; in the same way we must deal with our imperfections.

Sermon for the Feast of St. Blaise.

Self-love, self-esteem, and a false liberty of mind, are roots which can never be completely torn up out of the human heart. Yet, we may hinder the production of their fruit, which is sin. It is impossible, so long as we are in the world, to prevent their first sallies, their shoots, that is to say, their first movements; but we may moderate and diminish their number and their violence by the practice of the opposite virtues, and, above all, of the love of God. We must, therefore, be patient, and correct our bad habits little by little, conquer our aversions, and overcome our evil inclinations and passions according as they come into play. For we must remember that this life is a continual warfare, and there is no living creature

## Purification of the Soul

who can say, I am free from attack. Repose is reserved for heaven, where the palm of victory awaits us.

*Letter 769.*

Some authors assure us that if we write a few words on a whole almond, put it into its shell again, close it up very carefully and plant it, every fruit of the tree that comes from it will have the words written upon it. For my part, Philothea, I never could approve of the method of those who, wishing to reform a man, begin by the exterior, by the face, dress, or hair I think it much better to begin by the interior: "Turn to Me, says God, with your whole heart; my son, give me thy heart." For, the heart being the source of all actions, as it is, so are they. The Divine Spouse, inviting the soul, says, "Put me as a seal upon your heart, as a seal upon thine arm." Yes, truly, for whoever has Jesus Christ within his heart soon shows Him forth in his external actions.

*Devout Life,* part III. ch. 23.

Having found the Savior of our souls, Magdalen became so truly converted, that she was a pure and fragrant vessel, into which God poured the most precious and sweet smelling liquor of his grace, wherewith she afterwards perfumed her Savior; and she who by her sins was a mass of filth, became, through her conversion, a beautiful lily, a most sweet and fragrant flower; and the more foul and revolting she was before, because of her sins, the more was she purified and renewed by grace afterwards. just as we see that the flowers in the garden take their growth and beauty from putrid matter, and the more the soil is manured the more beautiful the flowers become, so in like manner St. Mary Magdalen, after her conversion, was more beautiful in her extreme humility, her fervent contrition, and the ardent love with which she did penance, because, before, she was so steeped in wickedness and sin. Sermon for the Feast of St. Mary Magdalen. Natural reason is a good tree that God has planted within us, and the fruits that it produces must be good. But in comparison with those that proceed from grace they are of very little value, but yet not without some value, since God has valued them and has given them temporal rewards: as, according to St. Augustine, he rewarded the moral virtues of the Romans by the great extent and glory of their empire.

*Love of God*, book XI. ch. 1.

The feelings of love that precede the act of faith necessary for our justification either are not true love, properly so called, or are an initial and imperfect love. These are, as it were, the first green buds which the soul shoots forth, when warmed by the rays of the celestial sun, as a mystical tree, in the early springtime, and which are rather the promise of fruit than the fruit itself.

*Love of God*, book II. ch. 13.

We may give an account of the order of the effects of Divine Providence, as regards our salvation, in descending from the first to the last—that is, from the fruit which is glory, to the root of this beautiful plant, which is the redemption of our Savior. The Divine Goodness bestows glory after merits, merits after charity, charity after penance, penance after obedience in following our vocation, obedience in following our vocation, after our vocation, and the vocation -after the redemption wrought by our Savior.

In fine, all these graces absolutely depend upon the redemption wrought by our Savior, who has merited them for us, according to strict justice, through his sublime and loving obedience, which made Him "obedient unto death, even to the death of the Cross," and which is the root of all the graces we receive, we who are spiritual branches grafted upon his stem. If, then, having been engrafted, we *abide* in Him, we shall, without fail, *bring forth*, by the life of grace which He will impart, the fruit of glory which is prepared for us (John 15:5). But if we are like dead boughs lopped off this tree, that is, if by our resistance we break the flow of his grace, it will be no wonder if at last we are cut off utterly, and, like useless branches, cast into the fire everlasting (John 15:6).

*Love of God*, book I, XII. ch. 5.

Theriacal wine is not called *theriacal* because it contains the real substance of *theriaca*, seeing that there isn't any in it. Rather, it is so called, because the vine plant having been softened in *theriaca*, the grapes and wine that are produced by it, derive from the *theriaca* virtue and efficacy against all sorts of poisons. If, then, penance, according to Scripture, saves the soul and makes it pleasing in the sight of God, and justifies it, effects which belong to love and seem to be attributable to it, we must not be surprised; for although love is not always to be found in perfect penance, yet its virtue and properties are always to be found in it, gliding in, as it were, through the loving motive from which true sorrow springs.

*Love of God*, book II, ch. 20.

A severe winter kills and destroys all the plants and flowers in the country, so that, if it lasted forever, they too would remain in this state of death. Sin, that sad and terrible winter of the soul, destroys all the holy works it finds there. If it always lasted, life and vigor would never come back. But, as at the return of the beautiful springtime, not only the new seeds, sown under the favor of this fair and fruitful season, shoot up fresh and strong, each after its kind; but also the old plants, which the sharpness of winter had nipped and withered, grow green and vigorous again. So, in like manner, when sin is driven out, and the grace of Divine love returns to the soul, not only the new affections which the return of this holy springtime produces, bud forth into rich merits and blessings, but the works faded and withered under the harshness of the bygone winter of sin, as if freed from their mortal enemy, resume their strength and vigor, and, as if raised from death, flourish anew and are fruitful in merits for eternal life. Such is the omnipotence of the Divine love, or the love of the Divine Omnipotence. "When the wicked turns himself away from his wickedness, and does judgment and justice, he shall save his soul alive. Be converted and do penance for all your iniquities, and iniquity shall not be your ruin, says the

*Purification of the Soul*

Lord" (Ezechiel, 18:27-30). And what means, "iniquity shall not be your ruin," if not that the ruins which sin has made shall be repaired?

*Love of God*, book XI. ch, 12.

THE VIOLET

## IV.
## PRACTICE OF A CHRISTIAN LIFE

**1.** *Faults to be fought against or avoided.*

T is quite true that sharp sayings and lively repartee make us often very vain, and that we turn up the nose of our mind more frequently than that of our face. We make eyes with our words as well as with our looks. It is not well to walk on tiptoe, either in mind or body, for, if we stumble, the fall is greater. Come then, my daughter, take good care to cut down little by little the overgrowth of your tree; keep that heart of yours lowly and humble, holding yourself quiet at the foot of the cross.

*Letter* 848.

If we are punctilious as to rank and title, besides exposing our qualifications to examination and contradiction, we make them vile and contemptible. For honor, which is noble when bestowed freely, becomes hateful when exacted, sought, and asked for. Flowers which are lovely so long as they are left in the soil wherein they were planted, fade as soon as they are gathered.

*Devout Life*, part III. ch. 4.

## The Mystical Flora

Slander that takes the form of wit is more cruel than all others; for as hemlock is not in itself a very speedy poison, but rather slow, and one for which it is easy to find a remedy, but, when taken with wine, it is beyond all remedy. In the same way, slander, which of itself would go in at one ear and out at the other, fixes itself firmly in the minds of the listeners, when it is presented to them through some keen and sprightly saying. "They have," says David, "the poison of asps upon their lips." The asp gives an almost imperceptible sting, and the poison produces a pleasing irritation which causes the heart to open and receive the venom, against which there is no longer any remedy.

*Devout Life*, part III. ch. 29.

Everything appears yellow to those who are suffering from jaundice. It is said that, in order to cure this disease, it is necessary to apply the remedy under the soles of the feet. Certainly, this sin of rash judgment is a spiritual jaundice which makes everything seem bad in the eyes of those who are afflicted by it. But, in order to cure it, the remedy must be applied, not to the eyes, not to the understanding, but to the affections, which are the feet of the soul. If your affections are gentle and kind, your judgment will be gentle and kind; if they are charitable, your judgment will be the same.

*Devout Life*, part III. ch. 23.

There are many different causes which serve to make us judge others rashly, and we must try to find them out, and correct them as speedily as possible. Some persons are sharp, bitter, and rude by nature, and make all that they meet sharp and bitter likewise, "changing," says the prophet, "judgment into wormwood, and never judging their neighbor but with rigor and asperity." It would be very well for these persons to fall into the hands of a good spiritual physician. For as this bitterness of heart is natural to them, it is hard to overcome it; and although it is not a sin, but only an imperfection, yet it is dangerous, because it makes rash judgment and calumny reign in the soul.

*Devout Life,* part III. ch. 28.

All Christians, certainly, and especially all religious, in considering and reading the lives of the saints, should try to conform themselves to their example, just as the bees only light upon the flowers in order to gather honey where with to nourish themselves. Now there are many souls who just do the very contrary of this, and resemble the wasps, who also land upon the flower, but to draw forth, not honey but poison, and if they do suck the honey it is only to change it into gall. Looking upon these actions of their neighbors, not to gather the honey of holy edification by the consideration of their virtues, but to draw poison from them by remarking the faults and imperfections of those with whom they converse, or even reading the lives of the saints, so as to find an excuse for committing the same sins and imperfections more freely. And, again, there are other malicious persons, who are not content with remarking other people's faults and copying them, but they put bad interpretations on all

## The Mystical Flora

they see, and excite others to do the same, so that they are exactly like wasps, who by their humming draw other flies to the flower where they have discovered the poison.

*Sermon for Palm Sunday.*

"It is better," says St. Augustine, writing to Profuturus, "to refuse entrance to the least semblance of anger, no matter how just. Having once let it in, it is hard to drive it out, and what was but a little mote waxes into a great beam."

*Devout Life*, part III. ch. 8.

"The field of the slothful man," says the sage, "is filled with nettles, and thorns cover the face thereof;" because he finds difficulties on all sides, and is always lamenting that he is obliged to labor so hard in order to acquire perfection.

*Sermon for the 1st Sunday in Advent.*

Sometimes we judge affection more by sheets of paper (in letter-writing) than by the fruits of true interior feelings, which only appear on rare and notable occasions, and which are more useful.

*Letter* 835.

The herb *aproxis* flames up as soon as it comes within sight of the fire. So it is with our hearts. As soon as they see a soul burning with love for them, they also become inflamed. "I will give way to it somewhat," one will say to me, "but not too far." Alas! You make a mistake, for this love is more active and penetrating than you imagine. When one tiny spark enters your soul, you will soon find that in one instant it will seize your whole heart, and reduce your resolutions to ashes and your reputation to smoke.

*Devout Life*, part III. ch. 18.

The walnut tree is very injurious to the vineyards and fields in which it is planted, because, being very large, it draws away all the sap of the earth, which is then not enough to nourish the other plants. Its leaves are so bushy and wide-spreading that they make a pleasant shade, and in fine it draws to itself the passers-by, who, shaking down its fruit, spoil and trample everything around. These foolish loves do the same injury to the soul, for they occupy it, and draw off all its thoughts and feelings so powerfully that it is not able for any good work. The leaves, that is to say, the conversations, amusements, and dallying, are so frequent that they waste all one's leisure, and then they cause so many temptations, distractions, suspicions, and other wretched consequences, that the whole heart is crushed and spoiled. In short, they banish not only heavenly love but the fear of God, enervate the mind, and weaken the reputation. They are, in a word, the sport of courts, but the plague of hearts.

*Devout Life*, part III. ch 18.

## The Mystical Flora

Although it is lawful to play, dress, and dance, see good plays and join in feasts and merrymaking, yet to have a great affection for these things is an obstacle to devotion, and is very hurtful to our souls. It is not wrong to take part in these amusements, but it is wrong to have a strong attachment to them. It is a great pity to sow such vain and foolish affections in our hearts. They occupy the place of good thoughts and impressions, and hinder the sap of our souls from being employed in good inclinations. Thus the ancient Nazarites abstained not only from all intoxicating drinks, but also from eating grapes, not because they could intoxicate, but because grapes might make them long to drink wine. I do not say that we are forbidden to make use of dangerous things, but I do say that we can never have a great affection for them without injuring our souls and impeding devotion.

*Devout Life*, part I. ch. 23.

"The great Saint Basil says that the rose amongst thorns makes this remonstrance to man: "The most agreeable things in this world, O mortals! are always mingled with sorrow; nothing here is pure: regret is always side by side with joy, widowhood with marriage, care with fertility, ignominy with glory, expenses with honors, disgust with pleasure, and illness with health. The rose is a beautiful flower," the holy man went on, "but it always fills me with sorrow, by reminding me of my sins, for which the earth was doomed to bear thorns."

*Devout Life*, part II. Ch. 13.

## Practice of a Christian Life

Let us leave this worthless world. Oh, may this Egypt, with its onions and its fleshpots, be loathsome forever in our eyes, that we may relish so much the more the delicious manna which our Savior will give us in the desert we have entered; and may Jesus live and reign in our hearts!

*Letter 883.*

Even the rose is not so perfect but that it has its imperfections, for although in the morning it is beautiful and brilliant, shedding a delicious perfume around it, in the evening it is faded and withered; so that the Scripture makes use of it to symbolize the pleasure and delights of the world, and things which, though they appear beautiful in our eyes, are fleeting and of short duration.

*Sermon for Palm Sunday.*

I say to you about dances, Philothea, what physicians say about mushrooms; even the best are good for nothing. If, however, we must eat mushrooms, we should take care and have them properly cooked. So, in like manner, if you are obliged occasionally to go to a ball, take care that your dancing be well seasoned. But how is this to be done?

By observing due modesty, dignity, and a good intention. Eat very few. and that not often (the doctors say in speaking of mushrooms), for no matter how well prepared they may be, too many are dangerous. Dance little, then, and very seldom, Philothea, for, if you do otherwise, you are in great danger of becoming fond of it.

## The Mystical Flora

Pliny says that mushrooms, being spongy and porous, draw towards them whatever is near them, and being near serpents, they are supposed to imbibe their poison. Balls, dances, and such nightly assemblies, draw towards them sin and vice, and excite quarrels, envy, jealousy, and foolish love-affairs. And as these exercises open the pores of the body, so in like manner they open the pores of the heart. By this means, then if a serpent approaching whispers a lascivious word, or some basilisk casts an unholy glance upon us, our hearts are more easily caught by the poison. Oh, Philothea, these recreations are generally dangerous; they dissipate the spirit of devotion, weaken our strength, I cool our charity, and waken a thousand bad affections within us. We must then be very prudent when obliged to take part in them. But above all, it is said that, after mushrooms, we must drink some generous wine. And I say that, after dancing, we should make use of such good and holy considerations as may prevent the dangerous impressions these pleasures may have made upon our minds.

*Devout Life*, part III. ch. 33.

### 2. *Virtues in General*

In tilling our garden we cannot but admire the fresh innocence and purity of the little strawberry, because although it creeps along the ground, and is continually crushed by serpents, lizards, and other venomous reptiles, yet it does not imbibe the slightest impression of poison, or the smallest malignant quality, true sign that it has no affinity with poison. And so it is with human virtues, Theotime, which although they are in a heart that is base, earthy, and engrossed by sin, are nevertheless infected in no way by its malice, being of a nature so frank and innocent that they cannot be corrupted by the society of iniquity.

*Love of God*, book XI. ch. 2.

Our miserable nature, wounded by sin, is like the palm-trees that we have in this country, which do not produce fruit but imperfect berries, mere attempts at fruit. Rather, to bear full-grown dates, rich and ripe, that is reserved for warmer regions, So our poor human hearts naturally produce certain beginnings of love towards God, but to love Him above all things, which is the true maturity of love due to the Supreme goodness, this belongs only to souls animated and assisted by heavenly grace, and who are in a state of holy charity.

*Love of God*, book I. ch. 17.

The pagan virtues are only virtues when compared with vice, but, when compared with the virtues of a true Christian, they do not merit the name of virtue. Yet because they have something of good in them, they can be compared to worm-eaten apples. With the color and a little of the substance of real virtues they have the worm of vanity concealed within them, and so are spoiled. For this reason those who use them must separate the good from the bad.

*Love of God*, book I. ch. 10.

## The Mystical Flora

The just man is like a tree planted near a running stream, which bears its fruit in good time, because charity watering a soul, produces within it virtuous works, each one in its season.

*Devout Life*, part III. ch. 1.

Man is only in this world as a tree planted by the hand of the Creator, cultivated by his wisdom, watered by the blood of Jesus Christ, so that he may bear fruits according to his Master's taste, who wishes to be served chiefly in this that we should, with our full consent, let ourselves be governed by his Providence, which leads the willing and drags the refractory.

*Letter* 860.

The vine branch united to the vine bears fruit not of itself, but because it forms part of the vine. Now we are united by charity to our Lord as members to their head. It is for this reason that our fruits and good works, drawing their value from Him, are meritorious for eternal life.

*Love of God*, book XI. ch. 6.

If you cut a rose-tree and put a grain of musk into the opening, the roses which come afterwards will have a strong perfume of musk. Cleave your heart then by holy penance, and put the love of God into the cleft, then graft upon this whatever virtue you wish, and your good works will be perfumed by holiness, without any more care about them.

*Love of God*, book XI. ch. 2.

The rod of Aaron was dry, incapable of bearing fruit of itself, but when the high priest's name was inscribed upon it, in one night it put forth its leaves, its flowers, and its fruits (Num. 17:8). We are like to this rod, dry branches, of ourselves useless and unfruitful, who "are not sufficient to think anything of ourselves as of ourselves, but our sufficiency comes from God, who has made us fit ministers" (2 Cor. 3:5), and capable of doing his will. And therefore, as soon as by holy love the name of our Savior, the great Bishop of our souls, is engraved on our hearts, we begin to bear delicious fruits for eternal life.

*Love of God*, book IX. ch. 6.

And as seeds that only produce of themselves insipid and tasteless melons produce luscious melons and muscadines when they are soaked in sugared water. In this way, our souls that could not conceive one single good thought for the service of God, when steeped in the sacred delights of the Holy Spirit, who is within us, produce holy actions which tend towards eternal glory, and carry us thither.

*Ibid.*

Our works, as coming from us, are only miserable

## The Mystical Flora

reeds; but these reeds become golden by charity, and with these is measured the heavenly Jerusalem (Apoc. 21:15), which is given to us according to this measure; for men as well as angels receive a greater or less degree of glory according to their charity and works, so that the measure of the angels is the same as that of men (Ibid. 21:17), and God will render to every man according to his works (Ibid. 22:12).

*id. id.*

Our works are like a little grain of mustard seed, and are not at all to be compared in greatness with the tree of glory which they produce. But, nevertheless, they have vigor and virtue sufficient to produce it, because they proceed from the Holy Spirit, who, by an admirable infusion of his grace into our hearts, makes our works his own, leaving them ours at the same time because we are members of a head, of which He is the Spirit, and grafted upon the tree, of which He is the Divine sap. And because in this way He acts in our works, and in a certain fashion we operate or co-operate in his action, He leaves for our part the merit and profit of our services and good works; and we leave Him all the honor and all the praise, acknowledging that the beginning, the progress, and end of all good that we do depends on his mercy, by which He has come to us and forestalled us, He has come into us and assisted us, He has come with us and conducted us, finishing what He had begun (Philip. 1:6). But oh! how merciful to us, Theotime, is God's goodness in this division. We give Him the glory of our praises, alas! and He gives us the glory of his joy, and so by these light and

## Practice of a Christian Life

fleeting toils we acquire everlasting goods for all eternity. Amen.

*Love of God*, book XI. ch. 6.

God has commanded us to do our very best in order to acquire virtue. Do not let us neglect anything that may assist us in this holy enterprise. But when we have *planted* and *watered*, let us not forget that God alone can give increase (1 Cor. 3:6) to the trees of our good inclinations and habits. For this reason, we must wait for the fruit of our desires and works from his Providence. If, then, we do not feel that we are advancing in the devout life so much as we desire, let us not be troubled, but remain in peace, and let tranquility reign always in our hearts. It is for us to cultivate our souls well, and to this we must apply ourselves faithfully. But let us leave the abundance of the harvest to our Lord. The laborer shall never be blamed for not having a rich harvest, but he certainly shall for neglecting to till his land and sow his seed at the proper time.

*Love of God*, book IX. ch. 7.

Do not be at all astonished if you do not see much advance in your spiritual or temporal affairs. All trees do not produce their fruit at one season, dear child. Those that bear the best are longest in producing them. The palm-tree takes a hundred years, they say.

*Letter to a Lady,* September 20, 1621.

## The Mystical Flora

Cherry-trees bear fruit very soon, because their fruit are only cherries that last a very short time. But the palm, which is the prince of trees, only produces dates, they say, a hundred years after it has been planted. A tolerably good life may be the work of a year; but the perfection to which we aspire—ah! my dear daughter, it can, in the ordinary course, only come after many years.

*Letter,* December 16, 1619.

Do not love anything too ardently, I implore you, not even virtue, which we lose sometimes by over-stepping the boundaries of moderation. I do not know whether you understand what I mean, but I hope you do. I am speaking of your longings and desires. It is not natural, it seems to me, for a rose to be white, for the red ones are more beautiful and have a more delicious perfume; but it is natural for the lily to be white. Let us be what we are, then, and let us be so, simply for the honor of our Creator, whose work we are.

*Letter to a Lady,* June 10, 1605.

I do not think it would be right to charge the Monasteries of the Visitation with practices which might remove them from the end for which God has established them. It would be very foolish to expect to gather figs off an olive tree, or olives off a fig tree. Whoever wishes for figs must plant fig-trees; whoever wishes for olives must plant olive trees.

*Letter to a Superior,* April 22, 1612.

## Practice of a Christian Life

We must take great care never to inquire why the Supreme Wisdom has bestowed a certain grace upon one person rather than upon another, or why it makes its favors abound in one place rather than in another. No, Theotime, guard yourself well against this curiosity. For, since all have sufficiently, nay abundantly, what is requisite for salvation, what right has any man to complain if it pleases God to bestow his graces more abundantly upon some than upon others? If anyone inquired why God had made melons larger than strawberries, or lilies taller than violets, why rosemary was not a rose, why a pink was not a marigold, why a peacock was handsomer than a bat, or why a fig is sweet and a lemon acid, we should laugh at such questions, and say, "Poor man, since the beauty of the world requires variety, there must be different degrees of perfection in all things, and one thing cannot be another. Therefore, some things are large, others small; some bitter, others sweet; some more beautiful, and others less so."

Now, it is the same with supernatural things, for "everyone has his proper gift from God; one after this manner and another after that," says St. Paul (1 Cor. 7:7). Thus, it is a great impertinence to inquire why St. Paul had not the same grace as St. Peter, or St. Peter the same as St. Paul; why St. Anthony was not a St. Athanasius, or St. Athanasius a St. Jerome. We might answer these questions by saying that the Church is a garden filled with a countless variety of flowers. There must, then, be flowers of various sizes, various colors, various scents, and in fine various perfections All have their worth, their grace, and their charm, and all in the assemblage of their

## The Mystical Flora

varieties form a perfection of beauty that is very agreeable.

*Love of God,* book 11. ch. 7.

### 3. On Virtues in Particular.

#### HUMILITY AND OBEDIENCE

Our first parents, and almost all others who have sinned, were led to do so by pride. For this reason our Lord, as the wise and loving Physician of our souls, goes to the root of the evil, and instead of pride He comes to plant. First of all, the very beautiful and useful plant of holy humility, a virtue that is all the more necessary because the contrary vice is so general amongst men.

*Sermon for the Purification.*

We must try to steep all our actions in the spirit of humility, hide our good works as much as possible from the eyes of men, and wish them to be seen only by God. But still we must not hamper ourselves to such a degree as to be afraid of doing anything good before others, lest we should be esteemed and praised for it. It is only weak heads that are sickened by the scent of roses.

*Letter.*

Humility, which hides and covers our virtues in order to preserve them, is ready, however, to bring them forth

## Practice of a Christian Life

when charity recommends this, so as to increase and perfect them. Herein humility is like that tree in the Isles of Tylos,[3] which closes its beautiful carnation blossoms at night, only opening them to the rising sun, so that the natives say that these flowers go to sleep in the night time. Just in this way humility covers and hides our earthly virtues and perfections, only displaying them at the bidding of charity, which, being not an earthly, but a heavenly virtue, not a moral but a Divine virtue, is the true sun of all virtues, over which it ought always to reign supreme. The humility that is injurious to charity is unmistakably false.

*Devout Life*, part III. ch. 5.

When the storm comes down into our valleys and between our mountains, it harms the little flowers, but tears the great trees up by the roots. It is the same with persons in high places—the higher up they are on the social ladder, the more trouble and inconveniences they have to suffer.

*Letters.*

Reputation is like snuff, which is useful when taken now and then in moderation, but which hurts the brain when taken too often and intemperately.

*Letters.*

---

[3] In the Persian Gulf.

## The Mystical Flora

Those who inhale mandragora from a distance, as they pass, enjoy a most delicious perfume, but those who breathe it closely and for a long time are made faint and ill; so honors afford a sweet consolation to one who tastes them lightly, without being engrossed in them too eagerly, while they are extremely injurious to the man who feeds on them and grows attached to them.

*Devout Life*, part III. ch. 4.

As the leaves of trees, which in themselves are not of much worth, are, nevertheless, very useful, not only for adorning the trees, but also for preserving the fruit while it is yet tender. In this way, good repute, which is not a very desirable thing in itself, is very useful, not only for the adornment of our life, but also for the preservation of our virtues while tender and feeble. The obligation of keeping up our character, and of being what people think us to be, urges on the courage of a generous heart with a strong and gentle violence.

*Devout Life*, part III. ch. 7.

Honor, rank, and dignity are like the saffron, which never thrives so well as when trodden under foot. Beauty, to have its full grace and charm, must be careless about itself; and learning becomes a discredit when it puffs us up, and degenerates into pedantry.

*Devout Life*, part III. ch. 4.

Do you know what we must do when we are

## Practice of a Christian Life

corrected and mortified? We must take this mortification like an apple of love, and hide it in our hearts, kissing and caressing it as tenderly as possible.

*Spiritual Conferences, 2nd Conference on Obedience.*

A rough file takes the rust off iron, and polishes it much better than one that is smoother and less rasping.

So it is with superiors, whose rule should always. Be fatherly and kind, but sometimes a little sharp and rigorous. See how sharp teasels are used to scrape linen, in order to make it fine; and it is with heavy blows of the hammer that the fine edge is put on the best sword blades.

*Letters.*

If God sees true lowliness in our hearts, He will bestow great graces upon us. This humility preserves chastity, and for this reason the beloved soul in the Canticles is called the lily of the valley.

*Letters.*

A true widow is, in the Church, as a little March violet giving out an exquisite perfume by the fragrance of her devotion, and almost always hidden under the ample leaves of her lowliness, and by her subdued coloring showing her spirit of mortification. She seeks untrodden and solitary places, not wishing to be disturbed by the conversation of worldly people, the better to preserve the freshness of her heart amidst all the glare with which

## The Mystical Flora

earthly desires of honors, wealth, and even love may surround her. "Blessed shall she be," says the Apostle, "if she remain s in that way" (1 Cor. 7:40).
*Devout Life*, part III. ch. 40.

Our mother is quite right in wishing for us a great humility, for it is the only foundation of spiritual life in a religious house, which never raises its branches or bears fruit until it has planted its roots deep in the love of humility and lowliness.
*Letter to a Superior of the Visitation*, December 16, 1622.

It is also the true spirit of our poor little Order of the Visitation to keep one's self very small and abject, and to esteem one's self nothing, except inasmuch as it pleases God to regard one's lowliness, while we esteem and honor all other ways of living in God. Now, as I have said to you, our congregation should hold itself among the congregations as the violet is amongst the other flowers—low, small, and subdued in color; happy, because God has created it for his service, and to diffuse a little fragrance in the Church. Everything that tends most to God's honor and glory must be loved and followed above all things. This is the rule of all true servants of Heaven.
*Letter*, October 15, 1614.

### CHASTITY

Chastity is the lily of virtues. It makes men almost equal to angels. Nothing is beautiful without purity, and human purity is chastity.

*Devout Life*, part III. ch. 12.

Consider how noble is this virtue, which keeps our souls white as the lily, pure as the sun, which makes our bodies sacred, and enables us to belong, heart, body, soul, and feelings, to the Divine majesty of our God.

*Letter,* March 18, 1608.

It is said that those who eat the herb called Angelica always have a pure, sweet breath. Those who have chastity, which is the angelic virtue, within their hearts, speak modestly, courteously, and purely. As for unbecoming and foolish things, the Apostle does not wish us even to name them, assuring us that nothing is so ruinous to good morals as evil communications.

*Devout Life,* part III. ch. 27.

The spouse in the Canticle of Canticles is represented with her "hands dropping with myrrh," a preservative against all corruption. Her lips are "bound with scarlet lace," the type of modest words. Her eyes are dove's eyes, clear and soft. Her ears are hung with ear-rings of pure gold, emblem of purity. Her nose is as the incorruptible wood of the cedar of Lebanon. Such ought the devout soul to be-chaste, honorable, and transparent in hand, lip, eye, ear, and the whole body.

*Devout Life,* part III. ch. 13.

## The Mystical Flora

St. Agatha, St. Thecla, and St. Agnes suffered death, rather than lose the lily of chastity, and we are frightened at mere shadows.

*Letter to St. Chantal.*

Avoid the company of impure persons as much as possible, especially when they are bold and shameless, as they generally are. Just as the goat by licking sweet almond trees makes them bitter, so impure persons can never speak to others without making them lose some of their innocence. They have venom in their eyes, and their breath blights like the basilisk.

*Devout Life*, part III. ch. 13.

Keep yourself always near to Jesus-crucified, spiritually by meditation, and actually by Holy Communion. For as those who sleep upon the plant called Agnus Castus become pure and chaste, so you will find that if your heart reposes upon our Lord, who is the true and immaculate. Lamb, your soul will be purified from all stains and imperfections.

*Devout Life*, part III. ch. 13.

While fruits are whole they can be kept, some in straw, others in sand, and some amongst their own leaves; but once they are touched in the slightest degree, it is almost impossible to preserve them without honey and sugar. Thus chastity, which has never been wounded or violated, may be preserved in various ways; but once it is encroached upon, nothing can preserve it but a spirit of true devotion, which, as I have often said, is the true honey and sugar of our souls.

*Devout Life*, part III. ch. 1.

As the most delicious honey is culled from the most exquisite flowers, so the love which is founded upon the highest and purest intercommunion is the best. And just as the honey brought from Heraclea in Pontus is poisonous, and makes those who eat it lose their senses, because it is gathered from a poisonous flower which is abundant in that country; so friendship which is based upon false and vicious grounds is always false and bad.

*Devout Life*, part III. ch. 17.

You will easily distinguish between a worldly friendship and one that is holy and virtuous, just as the honey of Heraclea is known from other honey. That poisonous honey is much sweeter than ordinary honey, owing to the aconite infused. And so worldly friendship is profuse in honeyed words, passionate endearments, flattery of grace and beauties; but holy friendship is simple, frank, and pure in its conversation, and can only praise virtue and the grace of God, which is its true foundation, and without which it cannot subsist.

*Devout Life*, part III. ch. 2.

Ah! is it not a pity that this balm of spiritual friendship should be exposed to the flies! This liquor, so holy,

## The Mystical Flora

so sacred, is worthy of very great care, in order to keep it perfectly pure and clear.

*Letter,* January 30, 1606.

### CHARITY—SIMPLICITY—SWEETNESS

It is said that those who have taken the antidote commonly called *St. Paul's Grace*,[4] never become swollen when bitten by a viper, provided the antidote be quite pure. In the same way, when our humility and sweetness are good and true, they preserve us from the swellings of pride and the burnings caused in our hearts by a slight or injury. If, then, when stung by slanders and uncharitable things, we swell up with rage, it is a sure sign that our humility and sweetness are not true and honest, but false and artificial.

*Devout Life,* part III. ch. 8.

If a vine is planted amongst olive trees, it bears rich grapes, that have a strong flavor of olives. A person who is often in the society of the virtuous cannot fail to share

---

[4] Editor's note: St. Paul's Grace is a medieval remedy, falsely attributed to St. Paul. It consisted of liquorice, sage, willow, roses, fennel, cinnamon, ginger, cloves, cormorant blood, and several kinds of pepper. It was mostly used to treat epilepsy, catalepsy, and respiratory as well as stomach ailments. Because it was also useful for wounds, it was thought to have uses against venom. These would not have been mixed together and taken all at once, but diluted and taken in stages as tinctures.

in their good qualities. By themselves the drones cannot make honey, but with the bees they help to make it. It is a great help for us in our devotion to converse frequently with devout souls.

*Devout Life*, part III. ch. 24.

God says as He does, and does as He says. And so, He shows us that we must not be satisfied with fine talking. Rather, we must add deeds conformable to our words, if we wish to be pleasing to God. And as with God doing and saying are the same, so our saying must be doing, and our words must be immediately followed by works. For this reason, when the ancients wished to represent a virtuous man, they made use of the comparison of a peach, upon which they laid a peach-leaf, because the peach is the shape of a heart, and its leaf that of the tongue, and thus they wished to show us that the wise and virtuous man has not only a tongue with which to speak well, but that he should never speak except as his heart wishes him to do. In other words, that he should never utter a word that does not come from the affections of his heart, which urges him to act up to what he says.

*Sermon for the Feast of the Purification.*

I recommend to you holy simplicity. Look straight before you, but do not look at dangers that you may see in a distance, as you say in your letter. They seem to you armies, and they are but rows of willows; whilst you are gazing upon them, you may make some false steps.

*Letter 842.*

## The Mystical Flora

In conversation take everything peacefully, my very dear daughter, no matter what is said or done. For if it is good, you have reason to praise God; and if it is bad, you may serve God by turning your heart away from it, without appearing either astonished or angry. You are not able to prevent persons who wish to say wicked things from saying them, and they will only say worse things if you appear to wish to stop them. In this manner you may remain innocent amidst the hissing of serpents, and, as a little strawberry, You will not suffer any contamination from slimy things creeping near you.

*Letter* 123.

It is troublesome, I admit, to guide particular souls, but it is a consoling trouble, like that of harvesters, who are never more pleased than when they are pressed down with work on account of the richness of their harvest. It is a toil that rests the heart by the sweetness which it brings to those who undertake it, as the cinnamon does to those who carry it in *Arabia Felix*.

*Devout Life*, Preface.

### PATIENCE

Look for a moment at a rose. It represents the glorious St. John, whose charity was brighter than the rose, which he furthermore resembles, because he lived amongst the thorns of many tribulations.

*Letter* 394.

## *Practice of a Christian Life*

Let us practice constantly that resignation and pure love of our Lord, which are never so perfectly exercised as in the midst of torments. For to love God in the midst of sweets, little children could do that; but to love Him in the bitterness of wormwood is a sure sign of our affectionate fidelity.

*Letter* 149.

### LITTLE VIRTUES

It is well to cherish many good desires; but you must be orderly in your desires, and make them come into effect, each according to its season and your power. Vines and other trees are hindered from bearing too many leaves and branches, that their sap and moisture may be sufficient to produce good fruit, and that all their natural strength may not go off in too great an abundance of leaves. It is well to prevent this multiplication of desires, lest our soul should amuse itself with them, neglecting meanwhile those practical things, the least of which is usually more profit able than great desires of things that are beyond our power. For God wants from us faithfulness in doing the little things which He puts in our power, more than ardor for the great things which do not depend upon us.

*Letter* 133.

The bees rifle the lily, and the iris, and the rose, but they also suck the smallest flowers, such as the rosemary

## The Mystical Flora

and the thyme. In this way they gather, not only more honey, but better honey, because in these little vases the honey is closer, and keeps better. It is quite certain that if we practice many small acts of devotion, we will also practice charity, not only much more frequently, but also more humbly, and, therefore, in a useful and holy manner.

*Love of God*, book XII. ch. 6.

Come, let us trudge on through these lowly valleys of humble little virtues, and we shall find the rose amongst thorns, charity which shines forth in the midst of afflictions from within and without, the lily of purity, the violet of mortification, and many more than I can tell. But, above all, I love these three little virtues—sweetness of heart, poverty of spirit, and simplicity of life; and these great exercises of charity-visiting the sick, helping the poor, consoling the afflicted; but all without flurry, and with true liberty. Our arms, as yet, are not long enough to reach to the cedars of Lebanon; let us content ourselves with the hyssop of the valley.

*Letter to St. Chantal,* September 13, 1605.

THE ORANGE-FLOWER

## V.
## PIOUS EXERCISES OF A CHRISTIAN LIFE

### 1. *Prayer, Meditation, and the Word of God.*

THE ancient philosophers, in speaking of man, said that he was a tree turned upside down, with its roots above, and its branches below. Now, as a tree cannot live long unless it continually draws its nourishment by means of its roots, so it is with man, who cannot live the life of grace if he does not draw down heavenly influences by means of prayer, which, after the sacraments, is one of the most powerful means, not only to preserve grace, but also to acquire it.

*Sermon on Prayer.*

As prayer places the understanding under the brightness of the Divine light, and exposes the will to the warmth of heavenly love, there is nothing that so completely frees the understanding from its ignorance and the will from its depraved affections. It is the water of benediction which makes the plants of our good desires grow green again, and flourish, which washes our souls from their imperfections, and quenches the evil thirst of passion within our hearts.

*Devout Life*, part II. ch. 1.

## The Mystical Flora

As the vintage is made by pressing the grapes, so the spiritual vintage is made by pressing the grace of God and his promises. To press the grace of God, we must multiply our prayers by brief but vivid dartings of our hearts towards God; and to press his promises we must multiply our works of charity, for it is in favor of these that God will fulfil his promises. "I was sick, and you visited me," He will say to us.

*Letter,* October 12, 1608.

Meditation is made, we may say, as the bees make honey. They make it by gathering the dew that falls from heaven upon the flowers, and drawing a little juice from these flowers, which they change into honey, and then carry to their hives. Thus, we go over and over the life of our Lord in meditation, taking up one action after another, and considering them, in order to compose the honey of holy virtues, and draw from them the graces of a holy meditation.

*2nd Sermon on Prayer.*

Meditation is like a person who smells a pink, a rose, rosemary, thyme, jasmine, and orange blossom, one after the other separately. But contemplation is like one who smells a perfume made from all these different flowers. For he receives at once the full scent of all the flowers which the other inhales separately, and it is quite certain that this perfume, which comes from the blending of all these odors, is more sweet and precious than the perfumes of which it is composed, taken separately one

*Pious Exercises of a Christian Life*

by one. After having drawn a great number of different affections from the various considerations of which our meditations are composed, we then unite the virtue of all these affections, and this union of their powers brings forth a certain quintessence of affection, more active and powerful than all the others from which it proceeds. While it is only one, it includes the virtues and properties of all the others, and is called contemplative affection.
*Love of God*, book VI. ch. 5.

The first condition necessary for praying well is that we must, in our humility, be little in our own eyes. The spouse in the Canticle of Canticles fills the angels with wonder, and makes them cry out in amazement: "Who is she that goes up out of the desert as a pillar of smoke of aromatic spices, of myrrh, and frankincense, and of all the powders of the perfumer, and leaning upon her beloved?" (Cant. 3 and 8). These words may well be applied to a humble soul who practices perfectly the beautiful virtue of humility; for although she may be very fruitful in good works, this lowly sentiment that she has of herself makes her see no good in herself; nay, she thinks that she does nothing, and seems to herself to be like a barren desert, which has no fruit-trees, because in herself she does not perceive a single virtue. And as this humility raises the soul nearer to God, it makes the angels say: "Who is she that goes up out of the desert?"
*Sermon on Prayer.*

The lily and the rose of prayer are only preserved and

## The Mystical Flora

nourished among the thorns of mortification.
*Letters.*

Those who walk through a beautiful garden do not like to leave it without gathering four or five flowers, to keep near them for the rest of the day, and to enjoy their scent. Thus, when our minds have been occupied with some mystery in holy meditation, we must choose two or three points which we find to our taste, and which may help us in our advancement in virtue, and remain with us during the day, to delight us by their spiritual perfume.
*Devout Life*, part II. ch. 7.

In leaving this interior prayer you must be very careful not to give a shock to your heart, for in that way you may spill all the balm which you have received from your prayer. I mean that you must try, if possible, to keep a little silence, and to pass gently from your meditation to your business, keeping the sentiments and affections that you may have conceived as long as possible within your heart and mind.
*Devout Life*, part II. ch, 8.

Imitate a little child, who with one hand holds tight to its father, while with the other it gathers blackberries from the wayside hedge. Even so, while you gather and use this world's goods with one of your hands, with the other hold always fast your Heavenly Father's hand, and look round from time to time, to make sure that He is pleased with what you are doing. And take great care, above all things, not to let go his protecting hand, for if He forsakes you, you will fall to the ground at the first step.

*Devout life*, part III. ch. 10.

It is said that the iris or water-flag shuts up at the sight of the sun, because the rays of the sun make its flowers contract and fold together; but when the sun disappears, they open out, and remain so all through the night. So, it is with this recollection of which we are speaking. For the very presence of God, the very feeling that He watches us from heaven or from any other place, although we do not really think of that other kind of presence by which He is within us, unites our faculties and powers together to reverence the Divine majesty, which love makes us fear with a fear that is full of honor and respect.

*Love of God*, book VI. ch. 7.

As the birds have their nests to retire to when they have need, and the stags their thickets, in which they can take shelter from the burning heats of summer, so our hearts, dear Philothea, should choose each day some resting-place, either on Mount Calvary, or in the wounds of our Savior, or in some other place near Him, where they may retire at will to seek rest and refreshment amid the toils of life, and to be as in a fortress, protected against temptation.

*Devout Life*, part II. ch. 12.

## The Mystical Flora

St. Frances of Rome, looking at a pleasant streamlet, as she knelt on its bank in prayer, cried out in ecstasy: "The grace of my God flows as softly and swiftly as this little stream." Another saint, looking at the trees in blossom, said: "Why am I alone without flowers in the garden of the Church?" Another, seeing some young chickens gathered under their mother's wing, exclaimed: "O Lord, keep us thus safe under the shadow of thy wing." Another, seeing a sunflower, said: "When shall my soul, O my God, follow only the attractions of thy goodness?" and taking a pansy, which is fair to see, but scentless, he cried out: "Alas! such are my thoughts; beautiful to speak of, but without effect or fruit." In this way you see, Philothea, how one may draw good thoughts and holy aspirations from everything that presents itself in all the variety of this mortal life.

*Devout Life*, part II. ch. 13.

I congratulate Madame N., to whom I say, that her retreat is like a date, which will, in the end grow into a beautiful palm of triumph. Yet, this may be only after a hundred hours, a hundred days, a hundred weeks, a hundred months; and the contradictions she has suffered may help her on to this.

*Letter to St. Chantal*, December 11, 1620.

For this reason, Theotime, amongst all virtuous actions, we must try to perform carefully those of religion and of reverence for Divine things. Those of faith, hope,

## Pious Exercises of a Christian Life

and holy fear of God, speaking often of heavenly things, thinking of eternity, aspiring to eternity, frequenting the churches and sacred services, reading devout books, and observing the practices of Christian life, for holy love is strengthened at will by these exercises, and sheds its graces more abundantly upon them than upon virtues which are simply human. In this way, the beautiful rainbow gives a sweet perfume to all the plants it shines upon, but more than all to the plant *aspalatus*.

*Love of God*, book XI. ch. 3.

The history, given in the sixth chapter of the third book of Kings, of the wonderful building of the temple of Solomon, says that there was only one entrance to the oracle, but this entrance had two doors of olive wood. For the present I will call the holy Gospel the oracle of Christianity. For in reality the oracle was nothing but the place where God showed his will to the people. And how are we taught, if not by faith, which may be called an oracle, because in it we hear God. *Fides ex auditu.* (Rom. 10). But the only entrance to this oracle is the Word of God, for we cannot enter this auditory of God, unless it is *per verbum Dei.* But this entrance has two doors-namely, that of the holy Gospel and tradition. They are made of olive wood, because they bear the grace of God.

*Sermon for the 4th Sunday after Easter.*

The doctrine of the holy Fathers is simply the Gospel explained, the holy Scriptures elucidated. There is no more difference between the Scriptures and the doctrine

## The Mystical Flora

of the Fathers than between a whole nut and a cracked one, of which one may eat the kernel; between a whole loaf and a loaf which is cut up and distributed to several persons.

*Letter on Preaching.*

The flower-girl Glycera knew so well how to arrange her flowers, that with the same flowers she made a great variety of bouquets. Thus the Holy Spirit disposes and arranges the lessons of devotion which He gives by the tongues and pens of his ministers, so that although the doctrine is always the same, yet the discourse is always different, according to the fashion in which it has been composed.

*Introduction to the Devout Life, Preface.*

Profane writers are good, but they must be used in preaching as we use mushrooms—very few of them at a time, and merely to excite the appetite.

*Letter on Preaching.*

You must not think it strange if I promise you water and roses, for these are epithets that suit every Catholic doctrine, no matter how badly it is arranged.

*Id. Id.*

Although all men are sinners, they are not all bound to be silent, and to abstain from teaching the Word of

## Pious Exercises of a Christian Life

God, but only those who lead a life quite contrary to this Divine Word. If, however, we hear it said and preached by great sinners, we must not cast it from us for that reason. But we should take it to ourselves, and do like the bees, who gather honey from all the field flowers. Although some are bad, and filled with poison, they, nevertheless, adroitly draw forth the honey, which, being a heavenly liquor, never mixes with the poison.
*Sermon for Passion Sunday.*

### 2. Devotion to our Lady and to the Saints.

Ah! when I remember that in the Canticles she (Mary) says: "Compass me about with apples," I long to give her my heart, for what other apple could this beautiful fruit-gatherer wish me to give her.
*Letter 97.*

I salute you, very dear daughters, in the love of the ever Blessed Virgin, upon whose cradle I invite you to throw flowers every morning during this holy octave; the lilies and roses of purity and ardent charity, with the violets of the most holy and most desirable virtues of humility and simplicity.
*Letter to a Superior of the Visitation,* September 7, 1616.

"You are a garden enclosed and sealed up," says the Spouse in the Canticles to the Blessed Virgin; a garden set with the most beautiful flowers that could possibly be found. And to whom belong all these fair flowers with which the Church is filled and adorned, if not to the Blessed Virgin, whose example has produced them all? Is it not through her that the Church has been sown with the roses of martyrdom—the violets of so many holy widows, who are humble and lowly as these flowers, but who shed a sweet perfume around them? And is it not to her that it owes so many beautiful lilies of purity and virginity, all white and innocent? It is after the example given by her that so many virgins have consecrated their hearts and bodies to the Divine Majesty by a resolution and indissoluble vow to preserve their virginity and purity.

*Sermon for the Annunciation.*

Does it not seem to you, my very dear souls, that it is to Mary we should apply these words of the Canticle of Canticles, in which the Divine Spouse, speaking of the beauties of his spouse in the minutest detail, says that her "head is like Carmel" (ch. 7). Mount Carmel is a very pleasant mountain, covered with sweet-smelling flowers, and the trees upon it shed around them the richest perfumes. But what does this mountain, these flowers, and these perfumes signify, if not charity, which, being like a beautiful and fragrant plant, brings forth all other virtues in the soul that possesses it, for it is never found alone? Although these words are applied to the Church, which is the true spouse of our Lord, and in which, as on another Carmel all kinds of sweet-smelling flowers abound-that is to say, all kinds of virtues, holiness, and perfections-they may, nevertheless, be very well understood of the Blessed Virgin, who is that one perfect spouse of the Holy Spirit, who possesses charity in so eminent a degree as to resemble Mount Carmel by the frequent acts of charity which she produces, so that this holy charity is like a beautiful tree planted in the midst of her heart, shedding delicious odors continually round her, and throwing out perfumes of incomparable sweetness.

*Sermon for the Visitation.*

O Mary and Joseph! peerless pair, sacred lilies of in comparable beauty, amongst which feeds the Beloved, who feeds too his loving servants: lilies with which the Sun of Justice, the splendor and brightness of the Eternal Light. is so sovereignly delighted, that in them He has displayed all the charms of his Heart's unspeakable love. Great father, St. Joseph, great friend of Jesus, great spouse of the beloved of the Heavenly Father, who wished his Son to "feed among the lilies" of these two most perfect spouses. I find nothing sweeter to my imagination than to see the celestial little Jesus in the arms of this great saint, calling him father a thousand and a thousand times, in his child like language, and with a heart all full of childlike love.

*Letter 690, to an Ecclesiastic appointed to a Bishopric.*

St. Joseph surpassed in purity the angels and archangels. For if the sun needs only a few days to give to the lily its dazzling whiteness, who can imagine to what an admirable degree Joseph's purity ascended,

## The Mystical Flora

exposed as it was night and day for so many years to the rays of the Sun of Justice, and of that mystical moon who borrows from the Sun her splendor.

*Conference on the Virtues of St. Joseph.*

You ask me, dear child, what bouquet you are to give to your valentine?[5] It must be made up of little acts of virtue, done in honor of this celestial valentine; and at the end of your meditation you should present it to him, that he may consecrate it to your dear Spouse. You may also cull your bouquet sometimes in the Garden of Olives, or upon Mount Calvary—I mean these bouquets of myrrh of your own St. Bernard—and you may entreat your heavenly valentine to receive them from your heart. And praise God for them, as if He shed their sweet perfume around, for you cannot enjoy the full fragrance of these Divine flowers or praise their sweetness enough. Nay, you may also beg of this good valentine to take your nosegay, and with his own hand hold it to you to smell in turn, and even to give you in exchange another nosegay. Ask him to give you perfumed gloves, covering your hands with acts of charity and humility, and also to give you coral bracelets and chains of pearls Thus must we cherish the tenderness of friendship with these blessed knights of the King of glory.

*Letter 793.*

---

[5] A saint drawn by lot and adopted as patron for the year, according to a pious custom established at Annecy by the holy bishop.

## Pious Exercises of a Christian Life

**3. Meditation upon the Mysteries of the Life of Our Lord and his Blessed Mother, our Lady.**

Above all things I commend to you earnest mental prayer, especially such as bears on the Life and Passion of our Lord. This is the tree of life beneath the shadow of which we must seek repose.

*Devout Life*, part II. ch. 1.

Be anxious, my very dear sister, to press this dear Savior close to your heart. Make Him be, as it were, a fair and fragrant bouquet upon your breast, so that everyone who comes near you may feel that you are perfumed, and that your odor is the odor of myrrh.

*Letter* 110, *to one of his Sisters.*

The vine is chiefly planted for the sake of the fruit alone. Therefore the fruit is desired and sought for first, though the leaves and the flowers come before it. So, the great Redeemer was first in the Divine intention, and in that eternal plan which Divine Providence formed of bringing creatures into existence. In the contemplation of this desirable fruit the vine of the world was planted, and the succession established of many generations, which, like the leaves and flowers, were to precede the fruit, as forerunners, making suitable preparation for that grape which the Spouse of the Canticles praises so much, and whose wine rejoices God and man.

*Love of God*, book II. ch. 5.

## The Mystical Flora

I have never found in holy Scripture that the palm was made use of to represent anything but perfection, and it always serves as a similitude for high and excellent things. It appears, then, that there is nothing vile or contemptible in this tree. Just as in the lily, above all the other flowers, there seems to be nothing low or abject, and I have never seen it used in Scripture, any more than the palm, except to represent perfection. This is not true of other members of the irrational or vegetable creation. In like manner, amongst rational creatures, the Blessed Virgin alone possesses in herself every kind of good, without any mixture of evil. She alone is free from the stain of sin and imperfection. She alone is all pure, all beautiful and immaculate, and thus it is said in the Canticles: "You are all fair, my beloved, and there is not a spot in you." (Cant. 4). She is a flower that has never withered or faded. But I speak only of mere creatures, for as to her Son, our Lord, He is not a mere creature, but God and man in one, so that in Him there could not be anything imperfect, since He is the source of all perfection.

*Sermon for Palm Sunday.*

It is then said of the Blessed Virgin, that she was in the city of flowers (Nazareth); but what was she herself, if not a flower chosen from amongst all other flowers, for the sake of her rare beauty and excellence—a flower which, by its odor of incomparable sweetness, has the property of producing many other flowers?

*Sermon for the Annunciation.*

## Pious Exercises of a Christian Life

"While the king was at his repose, my spikenard sent forth its odor." (Cant. 1). The spikenard is a little shrub which never raises itself aloft, like the cedars of Lebanon, but always remains in its lowliness, throwing out its perfume with so much sweetness that it gladdens all who approach it. Surely we may say with truth that the Blessed Virgin is like very precious spikenard, for she never exalted herself on account of all the great graces and favors which she received, or the praises which were given to her, but always remained beautiful in her lowliness and her littleness. By this humility, like the spikenard, she shed such sweet perfume around her that it ascended to the throne of the Divine Majesty. God was so pleased with it, that He descended from heaven, to come down here upon earth below, and to be incarnate within her sacred womb.

*Sermon for the Visitation.*

There are two kinds of flowers—namely, roses and pinks, which send forth their sweet scent in different ways. The roses are more fragrant in the morning, and before the sun is high their odor is sweeter and better. Pinks, on the contrary, are more fragrant towards evening, and their scent is then more agreeable. Truly, this glorious Virgin is like a beautiful rose amongst thorns, for though she sent forth all the times of her life an odor of very great sweetness, yet it was in the morning of her most holy childhood that she shed a fragrance marvelously sweet before the Divine Majesty. Oh! how happy are the souls who, in imitation of this

## The Mystical Flora

holy Virgin, consecrate themselves to the service of God from their childhood! How happy they are to have withdrawn from the world before the world knew them! They are like beautiful flowers freshly blown, that have not been touched or withered by the heat of concupiscence, spreading around, by their virtues and their purity, an odor of great sweetness before God. But to encourage the souls that have not had this grace, I am wont to say, that there are two kinds of childhood—the first is that by which we correspond promptly and fervently with the secret inspirations of God, when, at the first movement and attraction of grace, we leave all things generously to follow the inspiration. Certainly, if these souls walk faithfully in the way which our Lord points out, they will not fail to share in the feast which we celebrate today, in which this holy Virgin, in her tenderest youth and at the first bidding of inspiration, presented herself in the temple.

*2nd Sermon on the Presentation.*

The substance of honey which was in the manna represents to us very aptly the Divinity of our Lord, inasmuch as honey is a heavenly liquid. Now, though the bees gather honey from the flowers, they do not draw away the juice of the flowers. Rather, with their tiny little mouths they cull and gather up only the honey which falls from heaven with the dew. In the same way the Divine nature of our Lord came from heaven, and descended at the instant of the Incarnation upon that blessed flower, the most holy Virgin, our Lady, in whom the human nature, having received it, preserved it in the

## Pious Exercises of a Christian Life

hive of this most pure Virgin's womb for the space of nine months, after which He was born and laid in the manger, where we shall see Him tomorrow.

*Sermon for Christmas Eve.*

Imagine to yourself a large sponge which has just been created in the sea. If you look at it, you will see that there is water in all its parts, and that it is filled with water. The sea is above and below, and, in a word, it is surrounded with water on all sides; yet this sponge does not lose its nature, nor the sea its own. But remark, I beg of you, that while the sea is in all the parts of the sponge, the sponge is not spread through all the extent of the sea, for the sea is a vast and deep ocean, that could not be contained in a sponge. Now, this similitude remarkably represents to us the union of the Divine and the human nature. The sponge is the humanity of our Lord, the ocean his Divinity, which has so imbued the humanity that there is not the smallest part of our Lord's body or soul that is not filled with it. Nevertheless, the human nature does not thereby cease to be what it always was—that is to say, finite and limited, unable to equal the Divinity, which is an infinite sea, that comprehends and fills all things, but can never be comprehended or filled by anything.

*Sermon for Christmas Eve.*

Honey does not come from the earth, but from heaven, inasmuch as it is a liquid that falls upon the flowers with the dew. When it falls upon beautiful

## The Mystical Flora

flowers, it is preserved in them marvelously well, and the bees come to gather it with matchless industry and cunning, carrying it away for their nourishment. The Divinity is a honey come down from heaven upon earth into this beautiful flower of the sacred humanity of our Lord, with which it has been joined and united hypostatically.

*Sermon for Christmas Eve.*

I would fain know something about the conversations of these two great souls [Mary and Joseph going to St. Elizabeth's house on the day of the Visitation]; but I think that the Blessed Virgin only talks of that of which she is full, and that she only breathes of the Savior. St. Joseph, in turn, yearns also after the Savior alone, who, by secret rays of grace, touches his heart with a thousand strange feelings. And as wines shut up in cellars give forth the scent of vines in flower, so the heart of this holy patriarch gives forth unconsciously the odor and strength of the little Infant that flourishes in his beautiful vine.

*Letter* 896.

I leave you to think what good odor this beautiful lily-flower spread around in Zachary's house. During the three months that she was there, how each one was embalmed by it, and how, with few but very excellent words, she poured from her sacred lips honey and precious balm! For what could she pour out but that of which she was full? Now, she was full of Jesus. My God, I wonder at myself that I am still so full of myself after

## Pious Exercises of a Christian Life

having so often communicated. Ah! dear Jesus, be the child of our hearts, that we may breathe and feel you only everywhere.

*Same Letter.*

Good Jesus, how sweet this night is! All the heavens, as the Church sings, distill honey; and I think that these Divine angels, who make their admirable canticle sound on the air, come to gather this celestial honey on the lilies where it lies, on the breast of the most gentle Virgin and of holy Joseph

*Letter 869 to St. Chantal.*

I love to see the dear little infant in the manger, better a hundred times than to see all the kings upon their thrones. But when I see Him upon his holy mother's knees, or within her arms, with his little mouth like a little rosebud pressed against the lily of her holy breast, O God! I think He is more magnificent on this throne, not only than Solomon on his throne of ivory, but more so even than this Son of the Eternal Father ever was in heaven. For if heaven has more visible beauties, the holy Virgin has more of invisible perfections and virtues; and one drop of virginal milk which flows from her sacred bosom is Worth more than all the splendors of the heavens. May the great St. Joseph make us share in his consolations, and the sovereign mother in her love; and may the Divine Infant be pleased to fill our hearts with his merits forever.

*Letter 868 to St. Chantal.*

## The Mystical Flora

May this Divine Infant saturate our hearts in his precious blood, and perfume them with his holy name, so that the roses of holy desires that we have within us may be all purpled with its stain, and all fragrant with his ointment.

*Letter 897 to St. Chantal,* January 1.

O Jesus! fill our hearts with the sacred balm of your Divine name, so that the sweetness of its odor may spread itself over all our senses and in all our actions! But in order -that these hearts may become capable of receiving such a sweet liquor, circumcise them, and cut off everything that may be displeasing to your holy eyes.

*Sermon for the Circumcision.*

You are near that sacred crib, dear child, from which the Savior of our souls teaches us so much by his silence; and what is there that He does not say while saying nothing? His little heart throbbing with love for us ought, indeed, to set our hearts on fire. See how lovingly He has written your name in the depths of his Divine heart, which is beating there on the rough straw with the passionate ardor with which He desires your good. He sends up to his Father not a single sigh in which you have not your part, nor a single thought of his mind which is not for your happiness.

*Letter 871*

## Pious Exercises of a Christian Life

The magnet attracts iron, amber attracts straws. Whether, then, we are iron in our hardness, or straws in our lightness and worthlessness, we must unite ourselves to this little Infant, who is the true magnet of hearts.
*Same Letter.*

Keep very close to the crib during this octave of the Kings. If you love riches, you will find the gold they have left there; if you love the smoke of honor, you will find there the incense; and if you love the delicate pleasure of the senses, you will feel the fragrant myrrh which perfumes the whole stable.
*Letter* 882.

We can easily believe that the Blessed Virgin was so happy carrying Jesus in her arms, that her happiness prevented weariness or, at least, made her weariness delightful. If travelers who carry a branch of *agnus castus* are refreshed and rested, what refreshment must this glorious Mother have received from carrying the immaculate Lamb of God!
*Love of God*, book IX. ch. 14.

Let us consider that He is not only called the flower of the fields, but also the lily of the valleys. Everyone knows that the chief beauty of the lily is its whiteness. Now, who could doubt that this whiteness is to be found in all its fulness in our Lord, for He has always possessed a purity and whiteness so far raised above angels and

## The Mystical Flora

men that it is not capable of comparison. *Dilectus meus candidus*—my beloved is of unequaled whiteness (Cant. 5), says the sacred spouse in the Canticles, speaking of our Lord. And in the Book of Wisdom, Solomon says that He is the splendor of the eternal light, the spotless mirror of God's majesty, and the perfect image of his goodness.

*Sermon for the Eve of the Epiphany.*

The second quality of the lily is that, like the rose, it grows without cultivation or artificial means, as may be seen in certain countries. This shows us the love our Lord bore to simplicity, not wishing to be called by the name of garden flowers, which are cultivated with so much care and skillful devices.

*The same.*

And when He says: "I am the flower of the fields." He chooses the rose, amongst all the other flowers, on account of his love for poverty, for there is nothing poorer than this flower, since it has nothing but thorns, and does not need (as we have said) that people should busy themselves about it to cultivate it. The Spouse, wishing to praise his beloved, says that she is like a beautiful lily amongst thorns. *Sicut lilium inter spinas, sic amica mea interfilias.* And she, praising Him in return, compares Him to an apple tree. *Sicut malus inter ligna silvarum, sic dilectus meus inter filios.* (Cant. 11). My beloved, she says, is among the children of men like an apple tree among the thickets and forest trees. It is all laden with leaves and flowers and fruits. I will repose

## Pious Exercises of a Christian Life

under its shadow, and take the fruits that will fall into my lap; I will eat them, and will find them very sweet to my palate. *Sub umbra illius quem desideraveram sedi, et fructus ejus dulcis gutturi meo* (Cant. 11:3). But what is this apple tree of which the spouse speaks but the cross of the Savior? And in what orchard should we find it? It is without doubt on Mount Calvary, to which the spouse calls Him when she says: "Let my beloved come into his garden." (Cant. 5). For this is the place where that Divine tree was planted, and where we must search for it, to nourish ourselves with its fruit, and to keep ourselves under its shade. And what are the leaves of this tree? It is the hope that we have of our salvation by means of our Savior's death. Its flowers are the prayers which He made for us to his Eternal Father, and its fruits are the merits of his death and passion. Let us keep under the shadow and at the foot of this tree—I mean of this cross; let us sate ourselves with its fruit, and let us not depart until we are all steeped in the blood which pours down from it.

*Sermon on Prayer.*

As Elijah slept under the juniper tree, so we should repose under our Lord's cross by the sleep of holy meditation.

*The same.*

O my Jesus, beloved of my soul! Allow me to press your to my heart like a bundle of myrrh, and to kiss the foot of this holy cross, stained with your precious blood; and to promise You, that this mouth, which is so happy

## The Mystical Flora

as to kiss your holy cross, will abstain henceforth from all slander, murmuring, and lasciviousness. And my eyes, that have seen your tears, O Jesus! falling for my sins, shall never look at anything that is displeasing to Thee.
*Conference upon the Crucifixion of our Lord.*

Let Jonah rejoice in the ivy; let Abraham make a feast for the angels under the tree; let Ismael be heard from under the tree in the desert; let Elijah be fed under the juniper tree in the wilderness; but, as for us, we wish no other shade than that of the cross, no other feast than that which is there prepared for us. Thither we will address our tears and our cries; we wish for no other nourishment than the fruits of the cross. "God forbid that I should glory save in the cross" (Gal. 6:14). May it never then come to pass that we should glory in anything else!
*Sermon for the Finding of the Cross.*

It seems to me, in sooth, that I see Him, this crucified Savior, in the midst of your soul, like a beautiful tree of life, which, by the flames of the good desires that He gives you, promises to you the fruits of Divine love, which He usually brings forth in the places in which are found the dews of humility, with meekness and simplicity of heart.
*Letter 794, to a Religious.*

What do you think is meant by the palm-branch that we carry in our hands to-day? Nothing else but that we

*Pious Exercises of a Christian Life*

implore of God to make us victorious over our enemies by the merit and in virtue of the victory which our Lord won by his death on the tree of the cross.

*Sermon on Prayer.*

We consider the cross also, not as it is at present, separated from the Crucified, as a sort of relic, but as it was at the time of the Passion, when our Lord was nailed upon it, when this precious tree was laden with its fruit, when this myrrh distilled from every side in drops of saving blood. In this consideration our souls honor the true cross with the same honor wherewith they honor the Crucified, not so much relatively, but rather consequently and by participation or redundance.

*Standard of the Holy Cross,* book IV. ch. II.

The Roman writer, Pliny, describes to us an herb which is useful against the plague, colic, and gravel, and lo! We forthwith cultivate it with care in our gardens. Yet, perhaps, out of a thousand millions of plants of this species, there will not be three that will produce the effects ascribed to them by this author. We prize them all, therefore, because, being of the same species as these three or four which have produced the desired effect, we regard them as of the same quality.

Well, then! Our ancient fathers, spiritual botanists, have described the cross to us as a very precious tree, useful for the healing of our evils, and a safeguard against all sorceries and enchantments. They are our warrant for many sure trials and proofs which they have had of its

## The Mystical Flora

efficacy: why should we not prize all crosses, which are trees of the same species as those which have worked miracles? Why should we not pronounce them to be of the same quality and properties, since they are of the same form and figure? If the cross does not work prodigies on every occasion, it is not because it has not as much virtue in our armies as in Constantine's, but because we have not the dispositions which Christians had then; or because the supreme Physician, who applies this healing tree, does not judge it expedient to produce by it this effect. But without doubt, as by its form it always represents the Passion, it has always the same force also in itself.

*Standard of the Cross*, book II. ch. II.

Myrrh has a very sweet perfume, but its juice is very bitter. The dear spouse then (the Church or the devout soul) says that her beloved will be to her like a bundle of myrrh upon her heart, to show that she will always remember the bitterness of his painful Passion.

*Sermon for Quinguagesima Sunday.*

May our dear crucified Jesus be always as a bouquet upon our hearts! (Cant. 1:12.) Yes, for the nails that fasten Him are more desirable than carnation flowers, and his thorns than roses. Oh! my dear daughter, how I long to see you holy and all perfumed by the sweet fragrance of this dear Savior.

*Letter* 794

## Pious Exercises of a Christian Life

Here, then, is a precious balm to soften all your sufferings. Take a drop or two of the blood that pours from the wounds of our Lord's feet, and meditate upon them every day. In imagination, dip your finger into this blood, and apply it to your ailment, invoking the sweet name of Jesus, which is "as oil poured out," says the spouse in the Canticles (1:2), and you will see that your pain will be lessened.

*Letters.*

Look at St. Bernard, Theotime! He meditated upon the Passion step by step, and then, putting all the principal, points together, he made a bouquet of loving sorrow, and laying them on his breast, in order to turn his meditation into contemplation, he exclaimed: "My beloved is for me a bundle of myrrh" (Cant. 1:12).

*Love of God,* book VI. ch. 5.

Read, then, this book [of the cross], and there you will find the name of Jesus, which means *Nazarene*—that is to say, flowering—for by the cross our souls have been decked out with fair and holy flowers of so many virtues and so many sweet-smelling aureoles. It was there that our Lord became the rose of martyrdom, the violet of mortification, the lily of purity, being not only pure Himself, but purifying others. Our bed is strewn about and covered with flowers, says the devout soul, *lectulus noster floridus.* O beautiful hawthorn! upon your branches perch the birds of the Church, and there, meditating upon the wonders of God, they warble sweetly their holy

## The Mystical Flora

praises. *Absit mihi gloriari!* God forbid that I should glory save only in the cross of my Lord Jesus Christ.
*Sermon for the Finding of the Holy Cross.*

O God! what an unsightly vine is the cross, but how richly laden! There is only one grape upon it, but one that is worth more than thousands. How many seeds have holy souls found in it whilst meditating upon the graces and virtues which this Saviour of the world has displayed thereon.

*Letter,* October 12, 1608.

Speaking of the rod of Aaron, St. Augustine says that it resembled an almond-tree, and its fruit an almond, from which he draws a comparison that he applies to our Lord. He says that the almond is remarkable for three things: First, downy bark, which is good for nothing; second, a shell which surrounds the almond; and third, the almond itself. Now, in order to draw the almond and the shell from this outer bark, we crush and break it; and this represents very well our Lord's sacred humanity, which was so broken, crushed, and bruised during his holy Passion, and so much outraged that He said that He was not a man, but a worm trampled underfoot: *Ego sum vermis et non homo* (Ps. 21). The almond which is within the nut, and from which is drawn oil to give us light, represents the Divinity; and the shell, which is like wood, represents the cross upon which our Lord was fastened, and where his humanity was so broken and crushed by the torments that it suffered, that the Divinity gave forth abundantly the oil of mercy which has shed such light and brightness over all the earth, that the world has been freed from the darkness of its ignorance.

*Sermon for the Nativity.*

*Ego sum flos campi, et lilium convallium.* "I am the flower of the field and the lily of the valleys" (Cant. 2:1) But what flower of the field are You, Lord? Certainly when He says, "I am the flower of the field," we may understand the rose, because it excels all the other flowers in fragrance and beauty. Now you know there are two kinds of flowers: those that grow upon trees, and the others whose stock is an herb or plant. Amongst all those that grow in the form of. trees, the rose bears away the palm, just as the lily does from amongst those of the herb kind. The different qualities symbolized by roses and lilies are realized admirably in our Lord.

*Sermon for the Eve of the Epiphany.*

The first quality of the rose is that it grows without artificial aid, and has hardly any need of being cultivated, as you see roses in the fields growing up without any cultivation. And although its perfume is extremely sweet when it is fresh, yet it is much stronger when it is pressed and dried. And this represents marvelously well that Divine flower, our Lord, who came forth from the Blessed Virgin, as it had been foretold by Isaiah that a flower should rise out of the root of Jesse (Isa. 11:1). For though He gave forth perfumes of admirable sweetness all the time of his most sacred infancy and during the whole course of his life, yet it was at the hour of his holy death and passion that, like a rose crushed and withered by all, the torments He endured, He breathed forth a fragrance much more powerful in order to draw souls after Him by his perfumes.

The same.

The sweet Savior of our souls wished to be called Jesus of Nazareth, because Nazareth is interpreted flowery or flourishing city. *Ego sum flos campi.* "I am the flower of the fields," He says in the Canticle of Canticles. And to show us that He was not only a flower, but a bouquet composed of the most beautiful and sweet-smelling flowers that could be found, He wished to keep this name of Jesus of Nazareth upon the cross. But does it not seem that our Lord was more like a faded, withered flower upon the cross, than a blooming one? Look at Him, all covered with wounds, defiled with spittle, his eyes sunken and dim, his face bruised, pale, and discolored, from the greatness of his sufferings, all his blood poured out and the pangs of death having already seized upon all parts of his body. Oh! it was truly at that moment that He showed Himself rich in the flowers of all the most beautiful virtues. Oh! how great and lovely, my dear souls, are the flowers which this blessed plant of the death and passion of our Lord caused to bloom forth whilst He hung upon the cross. I will content myself with choosing four of the principal, most remarkable and most necessary in the spiritual life. The first is holy humility, which, like a violet, sheds around it a perfume extremely sweet in the death and passion of our Savior. The second is patience, the third perseverance, and the fourth is the very excellent virtue of holy indifference.

*2<sup>nd</sup> Sermon for Good Friday.*

Our Savior was Himself the sacrificer, who offered Himself to his Father and immolated Himself in love, to love, for love, and by love. But, nevertheless, Theotime, beware of saying that this loving death of our Savior took place after the manner of a rapture, for the object for which his charity bore Him to death was not so worthy of love that it could ravish this Divine soul which went forth from the body in a sort of ecstasy, driven forward by the great strength of its love, as we see myrrh sending out its first juice by its very abundance alone without being pressed in any way; and our Lord Himself said: "No man taketh away my life, but I lay it down of myself willingly" (John 10:18).

*Love of God,* book X. ch. 17.

Love makes the lovers equal. And so it is with Him, this dear Lover [Jesus Christ suffering]. He is the fire of love burning in a bush set with the thorns of pain, and I am at once the same, I am inflamed with love even in the midst of my afflictions, I am "a lily amongst thorns" (Cant. 11:1).

Ah! do not look at my bitter griefs only, but look at the beauty and charm of my love. Alas! He suffers intolerable pangs, this Divine and beloved Lover; and this it is that saddens me and makes me faint away with anguish; but He takes a pleasure in suffering, He loves his torments, and dies of joy at dying of grief for me. Therefore, while I grieve at his griefs, I am also ravished with delight at his love. I not only feel sadness with Him, but I place my glory in Him.

*Love of God*, book V. ch. 5.

If the prophet Jonah delighted so much in the ivy that our Lord had prepared for him, that the Scripture says, "Jonas rejoiced greatly in this ivy;" what should be the joy of Christians in the cross of our Lord, under the shadow of which they are sheltered much better than Jonah was under the ivy; they are much better protected and guarded by this sacred wood than Jonas was by the ivy.

*Sermon for the Finding of the Holy Cross.*

As the rainbow touching the thorny shrub *aspalathus* makes it more fragrant than the lily, so the redemption of our Lord touching our miseries, makes them more useful and delightful than original innocence would ever have been.

*Love of God*, book II, ch. 5.

There was, doubtless, very great joy in the ark of Noah, when the dove, which had gone forth a little before to see the state in which the world was, returned at length, bearing an olive branch in his mouth, which was a sure sign that the waters had ceased, and that God had given again to the world the happiness of his peace. But,

## Pious Exercises of a Christian Life

O God, with what joy, with what festive gladness, was the band of the apostles seized, when they saw the sacred Humanity of Jesus return amongst them after the resurrection, carrying the olive branch of a holy and agreeable peace, saying to them, *Pax vobis*—Peace be to you.

*Sermon for Tuesday after Easter.*

Have you ever happened, in some parched and sultry summer, to see your gardens gaping for rain, as it were with mouths wide open, and no relief for their thirst coming from the heavens? Did you notice how the herbs began to grow pale and dry, the flowers to fade and wither, the shrubs to seem as if dead? But, after a while, lo! There comes a hot, impetuous wind, which, gathering together all the exhalations that had mounted up, forms a thick, black cloud, that seems to veil all the sky. And within it the thunder broods and the lightnings flash, until it seems that, instead of bearing relief to the fruits of the earth, this dark cloud is going, with thunderbolt, and hail, and storm, to shatter the scanty remnant that the drought has left upon the earth, and so seems to threaten men with total ruin: when behold, suddenly, drop by drop, this cloud comes down in pure water, and gives drink to the thirsty fields according to their need, resembling rather a thick dew than an impetuous shower. And then we have good reason to praise God when we see the gardens and the fields grow green again, and greener than ever, the flowers again coming forth, and all the fruits and crops which could not breathe in the heat, taking breath again, and renewing for the poor sowers

## The Mystical Flora

the hope of the feast of a plenteous harvest. Oh! I have now given you, I think, a good idea of the mystery of this great day. The garden of the infant Church had remained already some time deprived of the living water, *quae est veluti fons aquae salientis in vitam aeternam*; that is, bereft of the sweet presence of its good Lord and Master. The fear and dread of Jewish persecution had dimmed these flowers, and withered and wasted all these poor plants, so that they might well say, " I have lifted up my hands to you to crave your help, because my soul, without your grace, is like dry and barren land that can bring forth nothing." *Expandi manus meas ad te, anima mea sicut terra sine aqua tibi.* (Ps. 142) All might cry thus except that blessed lily, the holy Virgin, on whom, by a special influence of Divine love, the dew of heaven continued always to fall in superabundance. They were all, then, together, offering up prayers to obtain the dew of the Holy Spirit, the Comforter, when, behold, this impetuous wind and this noise from heaven fill them with fear, and make them more and more send up sighs and prayers to the Divine Majesty. But this noise, this wind, this violence, in place of terror, changed soon into a soft rain of heavenly graces, which refreshed their courage so sweetly, that henceforth they spoke no more of dryness or aridity; for that happened to them which is said of the just man by the holy King David—that he will be like a tree planted by the running waters, which is always verdant, and will bring forth its fruit in due season. (Ps. 1).

*Sermon for Whitsunday*

## 4. Sacraments.

### CONFIRMATION

*Gifts of the Holy Ghost.*

"There shall come forth a rod out of the root of Jesse," says the prophet Isaiah; that is to say, the Blessed Virgin; and from the Virgin a flower, our Lord Jesus Christ. Upon this flower the Holy Spirit shall repose and communicate to Him "the spirit of wisdom and of understanding, the spirit of counsel and of fortitude, the spirit of knowledge and of godliness, and He shall be filled with the fear of the Lord." (Isa. 11). Thus, the sacred humanity of our Savior is like a Divine flower upon which the Holy Spirit has reposed to communicate to Him his seven gifts. This is aptly represented to us by the gold candlestick with seven branches, which hung before the Tabernacle of the Old Testament, and which might be called a flower, because these branches were arranged in the form of lilies.

*2nd Sermon for Whitsunday.*

### PENANCE

In order to wash away my past sins, I will accuse myself of them courageously, and will not leave one that I do not drive out. I will do all that I can to uproot them

## The Mystical Flora

entirely from my heart, particularly such and such faults which give me most trouble. To do this well, I will constantly embrace all the means that will be recommended to me.
*Devout Life*, part I, ch. 12.

Whilst our faults are in our hearts they are thorns, but, going forth by a voluntary confession, they are changed into roses, sweet and fragrant. As our own malice draws them into our hearts, so it is the goodness of the Holy Spirit that drives them forth.
*Letter* 819.

I wish you knew me thoroughly. You would not cease to have absolute confidence in me, but you would not esteem me much. You would say: Here is a staff upon which God wishes me to lean; I am quite safe, since God wishes this; but the staff is worth nothing after all.
*Letter to St. Chantal*, October 28, 1608.

### EUCHARIST

Farewell, my dear daughter; the bell hurries me. I am going away to the wine-press of the Church, to the holy altar, where this sacred wine is constantly distilled from the one delicious grape that our holy abbess [the Blessed Virgin], like a heavenly vine, has happily produced for us.
*Letter to St. Chantal*, February 21, 1606.

## Pious Exercises of a Christian Life

When several grains of wheat are pounded and worked together to make a single loaf, although they were before quite separate from one another, are afterwards so united that they can never be separated again. In the same manner the Christians of the early Church were so united, and had such fervent love for one another, that their hearts and wills were all mingled and confounded, but yet this holy fusion and commingling were not any hindrance to them. This made the bread, that was kneaded out of all these hearts, extremely agreeable to the Divine majesty. And again, we see that out of many grapes, all pressed together, one wine is formed, so that it is impossible afterwards to tell which portion of the wine is formed out of such and such bunches of grapes. Even so the hearts of these first Christians, in which holy charity and affection reigned, were all one mystical wine, composed of many hearts, like so many different grapes. But that which caused so great a union amongst them all was nothing else than frequent communion, and this coming to cease or to be rarely used, holy love has come thereby to grow cold amongst Christians, and has lost much of its force and sweetness.

*Sermon for the Third Sunday of Lent.*

If the most delicate fruit and those most easily spoilt, such as cherries, apricots, and strawberries, can be kept for a whole year by being preserved in sugar or honey, it is no wonder that our hearts, although weak and foolish, are saved from the corruption of sin when they are preserved by the incorruptible body and blood of the Son

of God, who is "sweeter than honey and the honeycomb."
*Devout Life*, part II. ch. 20.

## THE HOLY MASS

The Eternal Father receives the praises of others as the odor of ordinary flowers. Yet, when He perceives the glory and honor which our Savior gives Him, He, doubtless, exclaims: "Oh! behold the perfume of my Son's praises, like the odor of a field full of flowers that I have blessed."
*Love of God*, book V. ch. 11.

Prayer offered up in union with this Divine sacrifice has unspeakable power, Philothea, so, thereby the soul abounds in heavenly favors; as if leaning on her Beloved, who fills her so full with spiritual sweetness and perfume, that she resembles a pillar of smoke of aromatic spices, myrrh, and frankincense, and all the powders of the perfumer, as it is said in the Canticle of Canticles (Cant. 3:6). Make every effort, then, to assist every day at holy Mass.
*Devout Life*, part II. ch. II.

## MARRIAGE

Marriage is a state that requires more virtue and constancy than any other. It is a perpetual exercise of mortification, and will, perhaps, be so for you more even

*Pious Exercises of a Christian Life*

than is usual. You must, therefore, prepare for it with great care, in order that from this plant of thyme, in spite of its natural bitterness, you may be able to draw the honey of a holy life. May the sweet Jesus be ever the sugar and honey that will make your vocation sweet! May He live and reign in our hearts forever!

*Letter* 131 *to a Young Lady.*

THE PANSY

## VI.
## TRIALS OF A CHRISTIAN LIFE

### 1. *Tribulations.*

HIS life is such that we must eat more wormwood than honey. But He for whom we have resolved to cherish holy patience in the midst of all our troubles will give us the consolation of his Holy Spirit in his own time.

*Letter 867.*

No one shall be crowned with roses who has not first been crowned with the thorns of our Lord.

*Letter 211.*

As the juice of the vine, if left in the grape too long corrupts and is spoilt, so the soul of man, if left in its pleasures and its voluptuousness, in its desires and longings, becomes corrupted; but, if crushed by tribulation, it gives forth a sweet beverage of penance and love.

*Sermon on the Resurrection of Lazarus.*

How can we show our love for Him who has suffered so much for us, if it is not amongst aversion, repugnance,

## The Mystical Flora

and contradiction? We must thrust our heads into the thorns of difficulties, and let our hearts be pierced with the lance of contradiction. We must drink the gall and gulp the vinegar, and, in fine, eat wormwood, since it is God who wishes it.

*Letter 125 to a Lady.*

I will always take the part of Divine Providence, for it does everything well, and disposes of all things for the best. What a happiness for this young girl to be taken away from the world before malice had perverted her understanding, and to have left this mire before she was stained by it. Strawberries and cherries are gathered before pears or oranges; but this is because their season requires it. Let God gather what He has planted in his orchard; He takes everything in due season.

*Letter upon the Death of a Young Sister.*

I have noticed the temptation. Alas! my dear child, we must have some temptation. That one sometimes embarrasses the soul, but it never overthrows her, if she be a little on her guard, and brave. Humble yourself greatly, and do not be astonished. Lilies that grow amongst thorns are the whitest; roses near a stream smell the sweetest, and get the scent of musk. "What doth he know that hath not been tried?" (Ecclus. 34:9.)

*Letters.*

Thorns, according to the common opinion, are not only different, but quite opposed to flowers; and it seems that if there were none in the world, things would go much better for it. For this reason, St. Ambrose thought that only for sin there would not be thorns. But as there are thorns, the good husbandman makes them useful, and forms with them hedges and enclosures round fields and round young trees, to serve as a protection for them against animals. Thus the glorious Virgin, having her share in all the miseries of the human race except those which tend immediately to sin, employed them very profitably for the exercise and increase of the holy virtues of fortitude, temperance, justice and prudence, poverty, humility, endurance, and compassion. In this way, they offered no hindrance, but rather many occasions to heavenly love to strengthen itself anew by continual exercise and progress. In her heart Magdalen is not distracted from the attention with which she receives the loving words of the Savior by all the ardor and solicitude that Martha may have. She has chosen her Son's love, and nothing takes it from her.

*Love of God*, book VII. ch. 14.

The less there is of a private interest in the practice of virtues, the more does the purity of Divine love shine forth in it. The child readily kisses his mother when she gives him sugar, but it would be a sign that he loved her greatly if he kissed her after she had given him wormwood or chamomile.

*Devout Life*, part IV. ch. 14.

Just as the honey that is made from the flowers of the

thyme, a small and bitter herb, is the best of all, so the virtue that is practiced amid the bitterness of low and abject tribulations is of all the most excellent.
*Devout Life*, part III. ch. 3.

The crown of the bride ought not to be softer than that of the bridegroom. As the rose is among thorns, so is my beloved among the daughters (Cant. 2:2). It is the natural place for this flower; it is the fittest also for the Spouse.
*Letters.*

Love your cross well, dear lady, for it is all golden if you look at it with eyes of love. And if on one side you see the love of your heart dead and crucified amongst nails and thorns, you will find on the other a collection of precious stones, wherewith to compose the crown of glory that awaits you, if, while waiting for it, you bear lovingly the crown of thorns with your King, who has wished to suffer so much before entering into his joy.
*Letter* 143.

I know that your sorrows have been increased of late, and I have felt for you so much the more, although with you I praise and bless our Lord for his good pleasure which He fulfils in you, making you share in his holy cross, and crowning you with his crown of thorns.
*Letter* 149.

It is a good omen for this soul that she has suffered

*Trials of a Christian Life*

many afflictions, for, having been crowned with thorns, we must believe that she will be crowned with roses.
*Letter* 861.

God gives us great hopes that He is ours, and that we shall one day be wholly his. These successes at the beginning of our reformation, these fires, these irons, these beds of pain, this lameness, these contradictions—what do you think that all this is? Signs of God's love, signs of his good pleasure in us. He loves to rest upon the hawthorn of our affections. We wear his holy livery; let us be faithful unto death, and He will crown us without doubt in the kingdom of his glory.
*Letter* 75.

Plant Jesus Christ crucified within your heart, and all the crosses in this world will seem to you roses.
*Letter* 96, April, 1622.

Do you know what the shepherds of Arabia do when they see that a thunderstorm is coming on? They take shelter under the laurel trees, themselves and their flocks. When we see that persecutions and contradictions threaten us, we must retire with our affections under the shadow of the holy cross, by a true confidence "that to them that love God, all things work together unto good" (Rom. 8:28).
*Letter* 110.

Consider the pains which the martyrs suffered of old

## The Mystical Flora

and those that so many persons are now enduring, beyond measure much greater than yours, and say: Alas! My labors are consolations, and my sufferings are but roses, compared with what is endured by those who, without help, without alleviation, live in a continual death, overwhelmed with afflictions tenfold greater than mine.

*Devout Life*, part III. ch. 3.

How blessed are those who rejoice in afflictions and who change Wormwood into honey!

*Letter to St. Chantal*, August 14, 1609.

### 2. *Spiritual Desolations.*

There is great mistake into which many persons, especially women, often fall. This is to believe that the service which we give to God without any relish or tenderness of heart, is less agreeable to his Divine Majesty. On the contrary, our actions are like roses, which, although they are more beautiful when fresh, yet when dried have a stronger and sweeter perfume. In the same way, our actions performed with tenderness of heart are more agreeable to us who only look for our own enjoyment, yet, if they are done with dryness, they have more merit and value in the sight of God. Yes, dear Philothea, in a time of dryness our will carries us to the service of God as if by main force, and consequently it must be more vigorous and constant than in the time of tenderness and sweetness.

## Trials of a Christian Life

*Devout Life*, part IV. ch. 14.

Even when the rose is dried, it gives forth still a sweet and pleasing perfume. This confirms what I have just said of our Lord, who, although surrounded with crosses, thorns, torments, and all kinds of afflictions in his passion and death, nevertheless, sheds a sweet perfume around Him, to make us understand, that afflictions, interior darkness and troubles of mind, which are sometimes so great with the most spiritual persons and with those who profess devotion, that they feel as though they were almost entirely abandoned by God, are never capable of separating them from Him, since they can always shed the sweet perfume of a holy submission to his most holy will, accompanied by an unalterable resolution never to offend Him. All this is to be understood of the superior part of the soul.

*Sermon for the Eve of the Epiphany.*

The fire seen by Moses on the mountain represented holy love. And as these flames were fed amongst thorns, so the exercise of sacred love is maintained more perfectly amongst tribulations than in peace and contentment.

*Letter,* September 11, 1607.

I love your advancement in solid piety. This advancement requires difficulties, in order that you may be exercised in the school of the cross, in which alone our souls are brought to perfection. But I cannot help feeling that motherly tenderness that makes parents desire sweetness and comforts for their children. Be but courageous, my dear daughter. It is not with spiritual rose-trees as with those of our gardens. In the latter the thorns remain, the roses pass away; in the others the thorns will pass, the roses will remain forever.

*Letter* 144, *to a Lady.*

I see that all the seasons are to be found in your soul. At one time you feel the winter of sterility, distractions, disgust, and weariness, while at another the dews of the month of May, with the odor of the holy little flowers; and again, the summer glow of the desire to please our good God. There remains only the autumn, of which, as you say, you do not see many of the fruits. But it very often happens that in threshing the corn, and pressing the grapes, we find them more productive than the harvest and the vintage promised. You might wish it to be all spring time and summer; but no, my dear daughter, there must be vicissitude in the world within as in the world without. In heaven it shall all be a springtime of beauty, all an autumn of enjoyment, all a summer of love. Winter there shall be none; but here winter is necessary for the exercise of abnegation and of the thousand beautiful little virtues which are practiced in the time of barrenness. Let us keep on always at a quiet little pace; provided we have the will, good and determined, we cannot but go on well.

*Letter to St. Chantal,* February 11, 1607.

## Trials of a Christian Life

If you have but little gold or incense to offer to our Lord, you have at least myrrh, and I know He accepts it willingly, as though this fruit of life wished to be preserved in the myrrh of bitterness as much at his birth as at his death. In a word, Jesus glorified is beautiful, but although He is always very good, yet it seems to me that He is still more so at the time of his crucifixion.

*Letter to St. Chantal,* January 11, 1619.

## THE HAWTHORNE

## VII.
## DIVINE LOVE: ITS NOBLE PREROGATIVES AND SUBLIME ASPIRATIONS

1. *Nature, Properties, and Object of Divine Love.*

PON the sacred tree of the commandment, to love God above all things, depend all the counsels, exhortations, inspirations, and other commandments as its flowers, and eternal life as its fruit. Everything that does not lead to eternal life leads to eternal death. Great commandment, the perfect accomplishment of which endures in eternal life, nay, is nothing else than eternal life.

*Love of God*, book X. ch. 1.

The will, then, has a very close suitableness with good. This suitableness produces the complacency that the will experiences in feeling and perceiving good. This complacency moves and urges the will to good, this movement tends to union, and lastly, the will thus moved, and thus tending towards what is good, seeks all the means necessary for reaching to it. Now, generally speaking, love comprehends all this together, as a

## The Mystical Flora

beautiful tree, whose root is the suitableness of the will to good. Its foot is complacency, its trunk, movement, the seeking, pursuing, and other effects, its branches; but union and joy are the fruit.

*Love of God*, book I. ch. 7.

Basil, rosemary, marjoram, hyssop, cloves, cinnamon, lemons, and musk, joined together unbroken, form a very agreeable perfume by the mingling of their various scents, but not nearly so good as the water distilled from them, in which the sweetness of all these ingredients combines more perfectly into a very exquisite perfume, that penetrates the sense with a much keener delight than when their fragrance is inhaled in the other way. Even thus love may be fostered in unions in which both corporal and spiritual affections are mingled together, but never in such perfection as when minds and hearts alone, separated from all sensual affections, are joined together in pure spiritual love. For the fragrance of affections thus commingled is not only sweeter and better, but more vivid, more active, and more solid.

*Love of God*, book I. ch. 10.

Charity comprehends the seven gifts of the Holy Spirit, and resembles a beautiful flower-de-luce, which has six leaves whiter than snow, and in the middle the pretty little golden hammers. This gift of wisdom produces in our hearts a loving relish and delight in the goodness of the Father, our Creator, in the mercy of the Son, our Redeemer, and in the sweetness of the Holy

## Divine Life

Spirit, our Sanctifier.

*Love of God*, book XI. ch. 15.

The glorious St. Paul says: "The fruit of the Spirit is charity, joy, peace, patience, benignity, goodness, longanimity, mildness, faith, modesty, continence, and chastity" (Gal. 5:22-23). But see, Theotime, how this Divine apostle, counting these twelve fruits of the Holy Spirit, puts them down as a single fruit. He does not say, "The fruits of the Spirit are charity, joy," &c., but only " the fruit of the Spirit." Now here is the mystery of this manner of speaking: "The charity of God is poured forth in our hearts by the Holy Spirit, who is given to us" (Rom. 5:5). Yes, charity is the one fruit of the Holy Spirit, but because this fruit has an infinite number of excellent properties, the Apostle, who wishes to exhibit some of them by way of sample, speaks of this single fruit as if it were many, on account of the multitude of properties which it contains in its unity. On the other hand, he speaks of all these various fruits as one fruit, because of the unity in which this variety is comprised. So, too, one who would say that the fruit of the vine is the grape, wine, brandy, and the drink "that cheers the heart of man" (Ps. 103:15), would not mean that these were fruits of different kinds, but merely that though it is only one fruit, it has, nevertheless, many different qualities, according to the various ways in which it is employed.

*Love of God*, book XI. ch. 19.

## The Mystical Flora

We are forced, in order to speak of God at all, to use a great number of names, saying that He is good, wise, almighty, true, just, holy, infinite, immortal, invisible. And, indeed, God is all this together, because He is more than all this—that is to say, all this He is in a manner so pure, so excellent, and so exalted, that in one simple perfection He has the virtue, strength, and excellence of every perfection. Thus the manna was one food, which comprised in itself the taste and virtue of all other food, so that one could say that it had the taste of lemons, melons, grapes, plums, and pears. But it would have been truer to say that it had not all these flavors, but a single flavor, which was its own, and which, nevertheless, united all that could be agreeable and desirable in the various other flavors; like the dodecatheos plant, which, ancient writers say, cured all kinds of diseases, and yet was neither rhubarb, nor senna, nor rose, nor betony, nor bugloss, but one simple herb, that in its simplicity had as much strength as all the other medicines put together. O abyss of Divine perfections, how wonderful You are to possess within You in one perfection the excellence of all perfections, and this in so excellent a fashion that no one can understand it but yourself!

*Love of God*, book II. ch. 1.

The sun looks at a rose, along with a thousand millions of other flowers, just as much as if he looked at the rose alone. And God, though He loves a countless number of other souls, does not pour out his love upon one soul less than if He loved that soul alone, since the force of his love does not diminish according to the

## Divine Life

multitude of rays that it sends forth, but remains always full in its own immensity.
*Love of God*, book X. ch. 14.

### 2. Marvelous Effects of Divine Love.

All ought to serve charity, but she to serve no one, not even her beloved, of whom she is not the servant but the spouse. From her, therefore, we must learn the proper order in the exercise of the counsels, for to some she will prescribe chastity, and not poverty; to others obedience, and not chastity; to some fasting, but not alms-giving; to others alms-giving, but not fasting; to some solitude, and not the care of souls; and to others dealings with the world, and not solitude. In fine, she is the sacred stream by which the garden of the Church is made fruitful. Although she has herself only one colorless color, yet the flowers she produces have each its different color. She makes martyrs more crimson than the rose, virgins whiter than the lily; to some she gives the delicate violet of mortification, to others the orange blossoms of marriage, employing in various ways the holy counsels for the perfection of the souls that are so happy as to live under her guidance.
*Love of God*, book VIII. ch. 6.

Nearly all the plants with yellow flowers, and even wild chicory, which has blue flowers, turn themselves always towards the sun, and follow his course. But the heliotrope turns not only its flowers, but even all its leaves, according to the course of this great luminary. In like manner, all the elect turn the flowers of their hearts, which is obedience to the commandments, towards the Divine will. But souls that are greatly possessed by holy love do not only keep their gaze fixed on the Divine goodness by obedience to the commandments, but also by the union of all their affections, following the course of this Divine sun in all that He commands, counsels, or inspires, without any reserve or exception whatsoever.

*Love of God*, book VIII ch. 13.

Nazareth means flower. Oh! how well this city represents to us religious life. For what is religion, if not a house, or city, thickly strewn with flowers, since all the things that we do (when we live according to its rules and statutes) are so many flowers. Our mortifications, humiliations, prayers-in a word, all the exercises we practice what are they but acts of virtue, which are like so many beautiful flowers, that send up a perfume extremely sweet before the Divine Majesty? Therefore, we may well say that religion is a garden all sown with flowers, very pleasing to the sight, and very salutary to those who wish to inhale their fragrance.

*Sermon for the Annunciation.*

We may justly apply to religious persons what Jeremiah said of the figs which God showed him in a mysterious vision: " The good figs very good, and the bad figs very bad" (Jerem. 24:1).

*Letter to Clement VIII.*

## Divine Life

Know, my dear children, that if a grain of corn thrown on the ground does not die, it remains alone. But if it rots it will bring forth a hundredfold. Our Lord's word is here very clear, his holy mouth having itself pronounced it. Consequently, you who wish to wear the habit, and you who aspire to holy professions, examine carefully more than once if you are sufficiently resolved to die to yourselves, and to live only for God.

*20th Conference upon Religious Professions.*

As the olive tree, planted close to the vine, gives it its flavor, so charity communicates her perfection to the other virtues with which she comes in contact. But it is also true, that if the olive is grafted on the vine, it not only flavors it, but also gives it some of its juice. Do not then content yourself with having charity and the exercise of the different virtues along with it, but take care that it may be by it and through it that you practice those virtues, so that they may be justly attributed to it.

*Love of God*, book XII. ch. 3.

There are some virtues that, by reason of their natural alliance and correspondence with charity, are much more capable of receiving the precious influence of Divine love, and consequently the communication of its dignity and value. Amongst these are faith and penance, which, together with charity, regard God immediately; and religion, with penance and devotion, which concern

## The Mystical Flora

themselves with the honor and glory of the Divine Majesty. These virtues have so close a reference to God, and are so susceptible of receiving the impressions of heavenly love, that to make them participate in the holiness of that love, they only need to be near it—that is to say, in a heart that loves God. Thus, to give grapes the flavor of the olive, it is only necessary to plant the vine amongst olive trees. For without touching each other at all, merely growing side by side, these plants make an exchange of their qualities, so great is their mutual sympathy and fitness for one another.

*Love of God*, book XI. ch. 3.

All flowers, except a few of an abnormal nature, rejoice, open out, and grow beautiful at the sight of the sun, through the vital heat which they receive from its rays. But all yellow flowers, and, above all, those that the Greeks called heliotrope, and we call sunflower, not only rejoice at the sight of the sun, but follow with loving fidelity the attraction of its rays, gazing at the sun, and turning towards it from its rising to its setting. So all the virtues receive a new luster and excellent dignity from the presence of Divine love. But faith, hope, fear of God, penance, piety, and all the other virtues that of themselves tend particularly to God and to his honor, receive not only the impression of Divine love, by which they are raised to a high value, but they lean altogether towards Him, associating themselves with Him, following and serving Him on all occasions. For, in fine, dear Theotime, the Word of God attributes a certain power of saving, sanctifying, and glorifying to faith, hope, piety,

## Divine Life

fear of God, and penance, which shows us that these are very precious virtues, and that when exercised in a heart which has the love of God, they make it more fruitful and holy than other virtues, which of their own nature have not so great an affinity with Divine love.

*Love of God*, book XI. ch. 3.

I have seen at Tivoli, says an ancient author, a tree grafted in every possible manner of grafting. It bore all kinds of fruit, for on one branch there were cherries, on another nuts, and on others grapes, figs, pomegranates, apples, pears-in fact, every sort of fruit. This was wonderful, dear Theotime, but it is much more wonderful still to see in a Christian man Divine love, upon which all virtues are grafted, so that as one might say of that tree, that it was a cherry-tree, apple-tree, nut-tree, or pear-tree, so we may say that charity is patient, meek, valiant, and just, or rather, it is patience, meekness, and justice itself. But the poor tree of Tivoli did not last long, as we are told, for this great variety of production soon exhausted its vital sap, and dried it up, so that it died. Divine love, on the contrary, is strengthened and invigorated, so as to produce finer fruit by the exercise of all virtues; nay, as the holy Fathers remark, it is insatiable in the affection it has for producing fruit, and never ceases urging on the heart wherein it abides.

*Love of God*, book XI. ch. 5.

The fruit of a grafted tree is always according to what has been grafted upon it. If the graft is from an apple tree, it will produce apples; if from a cherry tree, it will produce cherries. Nevertheless, the fruit always keeps the flavor of the trunk. In the same way, Theotime, our actions take their name and their species from the particular virtues from which they spring; but from holy charity they take the flavor of their holiness, for charity is the root and source of all holiness in man. And as the stock communicates its flavor to the fruit produced by the engrafting in such a manner that each fruit still preserves the natural quality of the graft from which it springs, thus also charity infuses its own excellence and dignity into the acts of all other virtues. But, nevertheless, it leaves to each of them the special value and goodness which it has of its own nature.

*Love of God*, book XI. ch. 5.

All flowers lose their brightness and grace during the darkness of the night. But in the morning, when the sun makes these flowers visible again and beautiful, it does not render them, nevertheless, equal in their grace and beauty. And its light, spread equally over all, makes them bright band shining in unequal degrees, according as they are more or less susceptible of the effects of its splendor.

The sunshine, falling equally on violet and rose, will yet never make the beauty of the violet equal to the beauty of the rose, nor the daisy's grace equal to the lily's. But still if the light of the sun be very clear as it falls on the violet, and darkened with mists when falling on the rose, then, doubtless, it will render the violet more pleasing to the eye than the rose. Thus, my dear

## Divine Life

Theotime, if with equal charity one person suffers a martyr's death, and another the hunger of fasting, who does not see that the value of this fast will still not be equal to that of martyrdom? No, Theotime, for who would dare to say that martyrdom in itself is not more excellent than fasting? But if it is more excellent, charity entering into it does not take away the excellence which it possesses, but rather perfects it, and so leaves to it the superiority which it naturally has over fasting. Certainly, no man of sense will put nuptial chastity on a par with virginity, nor the good use of riches with the entire renouncement of them. And who would dare to say also, that charity superadded to these virtues takes away their properties and privileges, since charity has not an influence destroying and impoverishing, but rather sanctifying, vivifying, and enriching all that it finds of good in the souls that it governs. Thus heavenly love is so far from depriving the various virtues of the preeminence and dignity which they naturally possess, that, on the contrary, having this property of perfecting the perfections it meets with, in proportion as the perfections are greater, heavenly love raises them to higher and higher perfection; as the sugar in preserves seasons all fruits with its sweetness, but still leaves them unequal in flavor, according to the natural taste of the fruit, and never makes peaches or nuts so sweet or so agreeable as plums or apricots.

*Love of God*, book XI. ch. 5.

As in *Arabia Felix* not only aromatic plants, but all the rest, smell sweetly, sharing in this happy property, so in the soul that is inflamed by charity, not only the works that are excellent of their own nature, but even the smallest actions share in the influence of holy love, and are a good odor before the majesty of God, who, in consideration of these works, augments holy charity.

*Love of God*, book III. ch. 2.

Now, it is no wonder that holy love, being the king of virtues, has nothing, either great or small, that is not amiable, just as balsam, the prince of aromatic trees, has neither bark nor leaf that does not give scent. And what could love produce that would not be worthy of love, and tend to love?

*Love of God*, book III. ch. 2.

One of the properties of friendship is that it makes our friend and everything good that is in him agreeable to us. Friendship spreads its grace and favor over all the actions of him whom we love, however little susceptible they may seem of such a charm. The harshness of friends is sweetness; the sweetness of enemies is harsh and bitter. All the virtuous works of a soul that is God's friend are dedicated to God. For when a heart gives itself away, does it not give everything that belongs to it? When a person gives a tree, does he not give also the leaves, the flowers, and the fruits? "The just shall flourish like a palm-tree: he shall grow up like a cedar of Libanus. Planted in the house of the Lord, they shall flourish in the courts of the house of our God" (Ps. 91:13, 14). Since the just man is *planted in the house of our God,* his leaves,

*Divine Life*

flowers, and fruit grow there, and are dedicated to the service of the Divine Majesty. He is like "a tree planted near the running waters, which shall bring forth its fruit in due season, and his leaves shall not fall off" (Ps. 1:3). No, not only the fruits of charity and the flowers of the works which she orders, but even the leaves of the moral and natural virtues draw a special richness from the love of the heart that produces them.

*Love of God*, book XI. ch. 2.

As the rainbow, touching the aspalathus, deprives it of its own peculiar perfume, but gives it a more exquisite one, so when Divine love touches our passions, it takes away their earthly object, and gives them one that is heavenly. Our appetites may be made spiritual if, before eating, we thus excite a motive of love: " Ah! no, Lord; it is not to please this wretched creature, nor to appease this appetite, that I now seat myself at table, but in order, according to thy providence, to maintain this body, which You have given to me, subject to this misery; yes, Lord, for so it hath seemed good to You" (Mat. 11:26). If I hope for a friend's assistance, may I not say, "You have so arranged our lives, O Lord, that we must ask for help and comfort from one another; and because it pleases You, I will apply to this man whose friendship You have given me for this purpose." Is there any just subject of fear: "You wish me to be afraid, O Lord, so that I may take all proper means of avoiding this inconvenience. I will do so, Lord, because such is thy good pleasure." If the fear is excessive: "O God, Eternal Father, what need we, thy children, fear? What danger could come upon the little chickens sheltered under thy wing? Come, then, I will do what is right to avoid this evil, of which I stand in such dread; but after that, Lord, 'I am thine, save me' (Ps. 118:94); and no matter what may happen, I will accept it willingly, because such is thy good will." Oh, holy and sacred alchemy! O Divine solvent, by which all the metals of our passions, affections, and actions are converted into the pure gold of heavenly love.

*Love of God*, book XX. ch. 20.

### 3. *Mystical Transports of Divine Love.*

The herb *aproxis*, as we have said elsewhere, is so easily attracted by fire, that even when at a great distance it draws the flame immediately towards it, and burns away rapidly, catching fire not only from the heat, but from the mere light of the flame which is presented to it. When this great attraction, then, has united it to the fire, might it not say, if it knew how to speak: "My beloved fire is mine, because I have drawn it to myself, and I rejoice in his flames. And I am his, for if I attracted him to me, he has reduced me to himself, because he is stronger and more noble than I am; he is my fire, and I am his herb; I attract him, and he burns me." Thus when our hearts have placed themselves in the presence of the Divine bounty, and have drawn within themselves the Divine perfections by the delight they take in them, they may say with truth: "The goodness of God is all mine, because I rejoice in his excellence, and I am all his, since his good pleasure possesses me." Our souls, like Gideon's fleece, are filled with a celestial dew. And this dew is for

## Divine Life

the fleece, because it has fallen upon it, and in return the fleece is for the dew, because it is steeped in it, and derives its worth from it.

*Love of God*, book V. ch. 3.

"Let my beloved come into his garden," says the Spouse of the Canticles, "and eat the fruit of his apple trees" (Cant. 5:1). Now, the Divine Spouse comes into his garden when he comes into a devout soul, for since his delight is to be with the children of men (Prov. 8), where can He repose better than in the soul that He has made to his own image and likeness? In this garden He Himself plants the loving delight that we have in his goodness, and on which we feed our souls. As his goodness delights and feeds itself on our complacency, so in turn our complacency is increased by the pleasure that God feels in seeing that our pleasure is in Him. This mutual pleasure forms a love of incomparable complacency, by which the soul, the garden of the Spouse, from whose goodness it possesses the apple trees of delight, gives to Him the fruit thereof, since He is pleased with the complacency the soul feels in Him. Let us, then, draw God's heart within our own, and He will fill them with his most precious balm.

*Love of God*, book V. ch. 2.

Nature has so ordained that the heart of the mother, by its warmth within her bosom, should make the milk with which she nourishes her child; and so the mother's heart is truly the nurse of the child, feeding it with this

## The Mystical Flora

milk, which is the food of love. "Your breasts are better than wine" (Cant. 1:3). Remark, Theotime, that this comparison between milk and wine, made by the Divine Spouse, seems so true, that she is not content with making it once but repeats it three times. Wine is the milk of the grape, and milk is the wine of the breast. The holy Spouse calls her beloved a grape, but a grape o 'Cyprus, that is to say, of a most delicious perfume. Moses said that the Israelites might drink the purest blood of the grape (Deut. 32:14), and Jacob describing to his son Judah the fertility of his portion of the Promised Land, prophesied under this figure the true happiness of Christians, saying that the Savior would wash his robe, which means the Church, "in the blood of the grape" (Gen. 49), that is to say, in his own most precious blood. Now, blood and milk resemble one another as closely as verjuice and wine; for as the verjuice, ripened by the heat of the sun, changes color and becomes a pleasant wine, so blood, seasoned by the warmth of the heart, takes a beautiful white color, and becomes a nourishment suitable for the most tender infants. Milk, which is a soothing and loving food, represents the science of mystical theology, that is to say, the sweet relish which springs from the loving complacency that the mind receives when it meditates upon the perfections of the Divine goodness. But wine signifies ordinary and acquired science, which is drawn by force of speculation out of the wine-press of divers arguments and disputations. Now the milk that we draw from the breasts of the charity of our Lord, are worth incomparably more than the wine that we draw from human reasonings. For

## Divine Life

the milk has its origin in celestial love, which prepares it for its children before they think of it. It has a pleasing and delightful taste, its odor surpasses all perfume, it makes the breath sweet and fresh as of a new-born infant; it gives a joy without excess, and intoxicates without stupefying; it does not take away our senses, but exalts them.

*Love of God*, book V. ch. 2.

It was this love (of condolence), Theotime, that drew the stigmata upon the loving and seraphic St. Francis, and the burning wounds of our Savior upon the loving and angelic St. Catherine of Sienna, loving complacency having sharpened the points of sorrowful compassion, as the honey renders the bitterness of wormwood more sensible and penetrating, whereas, on the contrary, the sweet perfume of the rose is dulled and deadened by garlic planted near the rose-trees. For, as the loving complacency that we feel in the love of our Savior makes us feel more profound compassion for his sufferings, so, on the other hand, passing from compassion for his sorrows to complacency in his love, the joy is all the more ardent and more exalted. Then are exercised the pain of love and the love of pain. Then loving condolence and dolorous complacency, like Esau and Jacob (Gen. 25:22), strive which will make the greatest efforts, throw the soul into marvelous agonies and convulsions, and produce an ecstasy painfully loving and lovingly painful. In this way, those great souls, St. Francis and St. Catherine, felt a wonderful love in their sufferings, and inconceivable sufferings in their love, while they were marked with the stigmata, feeling a joyful love in enduring for their Friend, what our Lord felt in a supreme degree upon the tree of the cross. Here arises the precious union of our hearts with God, which, like a mystical Benjamin, is at once a child of pain and of joy (Gen. 35:18). It would be impossible to say, Theotime, how ardently our Lord longs to enter into our hearts by this love of dolorous complacency.

*Love of God*, book V. ch. 6.

A soul wastes away through pleasures, and a diversity of pleasures dissipates it, and hinders it from applying itself attentively to the pleasure it ought to take in God. The true lover has hardly any happiness except in the beloved. Thus all things were vile and worthless to St. Paul (Philip. 3:8), when compared with his Savior, and the Divine Spouse is all for her Beloved alone. "My beloved to me, and I to him" (Cant. 2:16). If a soul which is absorbed in this holy affection meets with creatures, however excellent, were they even angels, she stays not with them, except as far as is necessary to be aided in her search.

"Tell me, I conjure you, have you seen Him whom my soul loveth" (Cant. 3:3). The glorious lover, Magdalen, met the angels at the sepulcher, who, doubtless, spoke to her like angels-that is to say, very sweetly-wishing to comfort her in her sorrow; but she was so plunged in grief, that she took no pleasure either in their sweet words, or in the brightness of their robes, or in the heavenly grace of their bearing, or in the amiable beauty of their countenances; but, all bathed in tears, " they have

## Divine Life

taken away my Lord," she said, "and I know not where they have laid Him" (John, 20:13); and turning, she sees her sweet Savior, but in the form of a gardener, and her heart is not contented, for, all full of the love of her dead Master, she does not wish for garden-flowers or gardener. Within her heart she bears the cross, the nails, the thorns; she is seeking her crucified Savior. Oh! good gardener, she says, if perchance you have planted my well-beloved, my dead Lord, as a lily trampled and withered, amongst your flowers, "tell me quickly, and I will take Him away" (John 20:15). But He no sooner calls her by her name than, melting away with joy, "Oh, my God!" she says; "my Master!" Nothing, in sooth, could calm her down. She cannot be at rest with the angels, nor even with her Savior, unless He appears in the form in which He ravished her heart. The wise men from the East cannot content themselves in the beauty of the city of Jerusalem, nor in the magnificence of Herod's court, nor in the brightness of the star; their hearts search for the little cave and the little Infant of Bethlehem. The mother of fair love and her holy spouse cannot rest amongst relations and friends; they go on still, "seeking in sorrow" the only object of their complacency. The longing to increase this holy complacency cuts off all other pleasure, in order that the soul may enjoy more perfectly that to which the Divine goodness excites her.

*Love of God*, book V. ch. 7.

The soul that is strained and pressed by the desire of praising the Divine goodness more than she can, after many efforts goes outside oftentimes herself to invite all creatures to help her in her purpose. Thus the heavenly spouse, feeling herself fainting away with the violent efforts that she made to bless and magnify the beloved King of her heart, cried out to her companions: "This Divine Spouse has brought me into his wine-cellars" (Cant. 2:4), by contemplation, making me taste the incomparable delights of the perfection of his excellence; and I am so holily inebriated by the complacency feel in this abyss of beauty, that my soul languishes, wounded to death by the loving desire which presses me to praise for ever such transcendent goodness. Ah! come, I beseech of you, to the succor of my poor heart; sustain it with grace, prop it up with all sorts of flowers, compass it roundabout with apples, else it will fall fainting and languishing away (Cant. 2:5). This holy complacency draws the Divine sweetness into the heart, which is filled with so burning a love as to be wholly lost in its vehemence. But the love of benevolence makes our hearts go out from themselves, and exhale delicious perfume—that is, every species of holy praise; and yet being unable withal to mount as high as they would desire, "Oh!" they cry, "oh! that all creatures would contribute the flowers of their praise and the apples of their thanksgiving, their glory and adorations, so that on all sides we might feel perfumes shed around for the glory of Him whose infinite sweetness surpasses all honor, and whom we can never worthily magnify."

*Love of God*, book V. ch. 9.

Myrrh produces its first liquid as it were by perspiration; but in order that it may yield all its juices,

## Divine Life

it is necessary to aid it by an incision. In the same way the Divine love of St. Francis appeared in all his life as a sort of exhalation arising from him, for in all his actions he breathed nothing but this holy love; but in order to display entirely the incomparable abundance of that love, the heavenly seraph came to wound him. And to the end that men might know that his wounds were wounds of heavenly love, they were made, not with iron, but with rays of light. O true God, what loving agonies and what agonizing love! For not only then, but all the rest of his life, this poor Saint dragged himself along, languishing like one sick of love.

*Love of God,* book VI. ch. 15.

The blessed mother Theresa says admirably that when the union of the soul with God has reached such perfection as to hold us attached to our Lord, it nowise differs from rapture and suspension of spirit; but that, when it is brief, it is called only union or suspension, while, if long, it is called rapture or ecstasy. In effect the soul attached to her God so firmly and so closely that she cannot be easily taken from Him, is no longer in herself, but in God, even as a body crucified is no longer in itself, but on the cross, and as the ivy clinging to the wall is, no longer in itself, but in the wall.

*Law of God,* book VII ch 3.

Just as mariners setting sail with a favorable wind in good weather never forget withal the cables, anchors, and other things necessary in rough weather and in storms;

*The Mystical Flora*

so, too, although the servant of God may enjoy the repose and sweetness of holy love, he ought never to be without the fear of the Divine judgments, in order to use it amid the storms and assaults of temptation. Again, as the rind of an apple, which is of little value in itself, serves, nevertheless, greatly to preserve the apple which it covers, so servile fear, which is so little worth in itself with regard to love, is yet very useful in preserving love during the perils of this mortal life. And as in giving a pomegranate, we give it for the sake of the grains and delicious juice that it holds within, yet we also give the outer rind along with it; so the Holy Ghost, amongst its other gifts, bestows the loving fear of God upon the souls of the elect, so that they may fear God as their Father and Spouse, and gives them also a servile and mercenary fear as an appendage of the other, which is much more excellent.

*Love of God*, book XI. ch. 17.

### 4. *Consolations and Promises if Divine Love.*

Divine love is like the plant which we call angelica, whose root is as sweet-smelling and as useful as its stalk and its leaves.

*Preface to the Treatise on the Love of God.*

Now love is called a fruit because it delights us, and we enjoy its delicious sweetness as a true apple of Paradise, gathered from the tree of life, which is the Holy Spirit grafted upon our human minds, and dwelling within us by his infinite mercy.

*Love of God,* book XI. ch. 20.

In fact, holy love is a virtue, a gift, a fruit, and a beatitude. As a virtue, it makes us obedient to the interior inspirations that God gives us by his commandments and counsels, in the execution of which we practice all virtues, of which love is the virtue of all virtues. As a gift, love makes us pliant and amiable to our interior inspirations, which are, as it were, the commandments and secret counsels of God, in the execution of which we employ the seven gifts of the Holy Spirit, whereof love is the gift of gifts. As a fruit, it gives us a relish and an extreme pleasure in the practice of a' devout life, which requires the twelve fruits of the Holy Ghost, and for this reason it is the fruit of fruits. As a beatitude, it makes us take as a great favor and singular honor, the affronts, slanders, reproaches, and insults, which the world offers to us, and it makes us renounce and reject all other glory but that which proceeds from our beloved Crucified Savior, for whom we glory in abjection, abnegation, and the annihilation of ourselves, wishing no other sign of majesty than the thorny crown of the Crucified, the scepter of his reed, the robe of scorn which they put upon Him, and the throne of the cross, on which loving, holy souls have more contentment, joy, glory, and happiness, than ever Solomon had on his ivory throne. Love is often represented by the pomegranate, which, drawing its properties from the tree, can be called the virtue of the tree, as it seems also to be its gift which it bestows upon man, and its fruit, since it is eaten to please man's taste;

and finally, it is the glory, so to speak, and beatitude of the tree, since it bears the crown and diadem.

*Love of God*, book XI. ch. 19.

There is a certain herb, which, if chewed, imparts so great a sweetness, that they who keep it in their mouth cannot hunger or thirst. Even so, those to whom God gives his heavenly manna of interior sweetness and consolation, can neither desire nor accept worldly consolations with any real zest or satisfaction. It is a little foretaste of eternal blessedness, which God gives to those who seek Him. It is the sugar-plum which He gives to his little children to attract them, and the cordial which He presents to them to strengthen their hearts, lastly, it is sometimes also the pledge and earnest of the eternal rewards.

*Devout Life*, part IV. ch. 14.

Those who hold in their mouths a certain herb called *scitica*, feel neither hunger nor thirst, it satisfies them so completely, and yet they never lose their appetite, it nourishes them so deliciously. When our will has found God, it rests in Him, taking in Him a sovereign complacency, and nevertheless, it fails not to exercise the movement of desire. For as it desires to love, it loves also to desire, it has the desire of love and the love of desire. The heart's repose does not consist in remaining motionless, but in needing nothing. It lies not in having no motion but in being under no necessity to move.

*Love of God*, book IV. ch. 3.

## *Divine Life*

Nothing makes one find chamomile so bitter as to take honey beforehand. When we come to relish Divine things, it will be no longer possible for the things of this world to excite our appetite.

*Letter* 114.

You have surfeited yourself with worldly pleasures; no wonder that spiritual delights are repulsive to you. "To the overfed dove even cherries are bitter," says the old proverb. And our Lady says, "He hath filled the hungry with good things, but the rich He hath sent empty away." They who abound in worldly pleasures are incapable of such as are spiritual.

*Devout Life*, book IV, ch. 14.

The pomegranate, by its bright, red color, by the number of its closely serried grains, and by its beautiful corolla, aptly symbolizes, says St. Gregory, holy charity, which is all crimson in the ardor of its love for God, adorned with a variety of virtues, and bearing the crown of the everlasting recompense. But the juice of the pomegranate, which is, we all know, very agreeable to both the sick and the healthy, is so mixed up with bitterness and sweetness, that it is hard to tell whether it pleases the palate by its sweetish bitterness or by its bitter sweetness. Just so, Theotime, love is bitter-sweet, and as long as we are in this world its sweetness is never perfectly sweet, because love itself is never perfect, and never purely and perfectly sated and satisfied.

## The Mystical Flora

Nevertheless, love is even here exceedingly pleasing, its bitterness rendering more delicate the suavity of its sweetness, while its sweetness makes the charm of its bitterness keener.

*Love of God*, book VI. ch. 13.

Oh! let us love perfectly this Divine being, who prepares for us so much sweetness in heaven. Let us be all for Him; and let us journey on, night and day, through thorns and roses, to reach this heavenly Jerusalem.

*Letter 213 to St. Chantal.*

My beloved, says the spouse of the Canticles, is to me a bundle of myrrh. I will take Him and place Him in the midst of my heart and my affections, so that the drops of this myrrh, falling upon them, will make them strong and firm amidst all tribulations.

*Sermon for 2nd Sunday after Epiphany.*

It will come, the hour of consolation, and then, with unspeakable sweetness of soul, you will lay your interior open before the Divine Goodness, which will change your rocks into streams of water, your serpent into a rod, and all the thorns of your heart into roses, and the richest of roses, which will refresh your spirit with their sweetness.

*Letters.*

Take care, if there come to you some inward relish or

## Divine Life

caress of our Lord, not to attach yourself to it. It is like the sweet ingredients that the apothecary puts in the bitter dose for the sick person. The sick person must swallow the bitter medicine for his health's sake, and, though the apothecary may sweeten it thus, the patient must feel afterwards the bitter effects of the medicine.

*Conference* 20.

Though the palm is the prince of trees, it is yet the humblest. It shows this by hiding its flowers in spring time when all other trees let theirs be seen, and by only allowing them to appear in the great heats. The palm keeps its leaves shut up in pouches made in the form of cases or sheaths. All this represents to us very well the difference between souls that aim at perfection and other souls that do not, the difference between the just and those who live according to the world; for worldly and earthly men, who live according to the ways of earth, as soon as they have some good thought, or some idea that seems to them worthy of being esteemed, or if they have some virtue, are never at rest until they have exhibited it, and made it known to everyone they meet. Wherein they run the same risk as the trees which are very early in sending out their leaves in the spring, like the almond trees: for if, perchance, the frost surprises them, they perish, and bear no fruit. Worldly persons, who so lightly allow their flowers to open out in the spring-time of this mortal life, by a spirit of pride and ambition, run always a great risk of being caught in the frost, which will make them lose the fruit of their actions. The just, on the contrary, keep all their flowers enclosed in the sheath of

## The Mystical Flora

holy humility, and do not, as far as they can, allow them to appear until the time of great heat. When God, the Divine Sun of justice, will come to warm their hearts in eternal life, where they will bear forever the sweet fruit of happiness and immortality.

*Virtues of St. Joseph*, 19th Conference.

We are like coral, which, in the place of its origin, the ocean, is a pale green shrub, weak and pliable; but once it is taken out of the depth of the sea, as out of the womb of its mother, it becomes almost a stone, and changes from green to a rich red. Thus when we are immersed in the sea of this world, the place of our birth, we are subject to extreme vicissitudes, and pliable on every hand—on the right, to heavenly love by inspiration; on the left, to earthly love by temptation. But if once drawn out of this mortality, we have changed the pale green of our timorous hopes into the rich red of secure enjoyment; never more shall we be changeable, but shall abide forever fixed in love eternal.

*Love of God*, book IV. ch. 1.

St. Gregory the Great, wishing in his Dialogues to tell us of the marvelous things of the other world, makes use of these words: Imagine to yourself, he says, a woman who is cast into a dark prison just before the birth of her child, and, after he is born, is condemned to remain there the rest of her days, and there to bring up her child. When this child is growing up, his poor mother, wishing to make him understand the beauty of the hills covered

## Divine Life

with a great variety of fruits, oranges, lemons, pears, apples, and so forth, shows him a few leaves of these trees, and says to him: "My child, these trees are covered with leaves like this." Then, showing him an apple or an orange, which she holds in her hand, "And they are laden with fruits like this; are they not fair to see?" she says. Yet the child knows not what all this means, but remains still in his ignorance, unable still to understand, from what his mother says to him or shows to him, how all these things are made, such a mere nothing is all this compared with what these things are in reality. It is just the same with all the things that we could say about the grandeur and glory and happiness everlasting, and about the beauty and pleasantness with which heaven is filled; for between the one leaf and the one fruit of the tree and the tree itself, when covered with leaves and laden with fruits all together; or, again, between what the mother tells her child and what he understands of it, there is even more proportion than there is between the light of the sun and the brightness which the blessed enjoy in glory; neither the beauty of the meadows decked with flowers in spring, nor the pleasantness of the fields covered with the ripe harvests, being fit to compare with the beauty and pleasantness of the celestial fields of eternal happiness, which surpass infinitely all that could be said of them or conceived.

*Sermon for 2nd Sunday of Lent.*

Oh, dear resolutions, you are the beautiful tree of life, which my God has planted with his own hand in the midst of my heart, and which my Savior wishes to water

## The Mystical Flora

with his blood to make it bear fruit. I would die a thousand deaths rather than suffer any wind to uproot you from my heart. No; neither delights, nor riches, nor tribulations shall ever tear me from this resolve. Ah! Lord, Thou hast planted it, and in thy Fatherly bosom Thou hast from eternity kept this beautiful tree for my garden. Alas! how many souls there are who have not been favored thus! And how then can I ever humble myself enough beneath thy mercy?

*Devout Life,* part V. ch. 15.

FINIS

www.ingramcontent.com/pod-product-compliance
Lightning Source LLC
Chambersburg PA
CBHW011405070526
44577CB00004B/408